Just Up the Road:
Child Abuse in Rural
America

∿

Crystal Daniels Weible
2012

Just Up The Road

Dedicated to my father, Dale H. Daniels
1927-2012

Just Up The Road

Crystal Daniels Weible

Acknowledgements

✿

For the children that allowed me to be a part of their lives and to the people that love them, including my many co-workers, and most especially, Brenda Yeager. For my own children, Sarah, Adam, Mary, Sam, Anna, Ben, Abby and Hiram, I am honored to be your mother. To my beautiful grandchildren, Brody, Rylee, Campbell, Luke, Lilly and Jane, who bring me joy. For my parents, Dale and Phyllis Daniels, who raised me to work hard, share and be kind to others. To my friends that suffered through the readings, gave suggestions and to the man that puts up with me, I love you.

To the unsung heroes that fight the fight every day: Judges, Prosecutors, CASA volunteers and Social Workers. If you can save one life, you save generations to come. Lest anyone forget the dangers of being a social worker, Brenda Yeager and others involved are real. Other names have been changed or deleted in order to protect those children and families that have been given the opportunity to change. There is always hope...

A special thank you to Ed Dawson, Editor of the Herald-Dispatch who said I could use these pictures and articles and to those that worked hard to make sure child abuse and neglect were not overlooked through their photography and writing.

~ 1 ~

Just Up The Road

These are just a few stories. Multiply those by thousands and you may begin to understand the significance of child abuse. Any errors, mistakes, omissions and or opinions are all my own.

Forward

꙳

Every day, thousands of children move from one place to another because their lives are transient and permanency is non-existent. They move because their caregiver has been evicted for not paying rent, for using drugs, or for breaking a rule in government housing. They move so often that boxes or garbage bags are their dressers and clothes spill out on dirty floors. Many have moved so frequently, that they may have attended three or more schools in one year, and few can remember the names of the schools or the friends they started to make.

Sometimes a move is thought necessary if a parent or caregiver feels that Child Protective Services is looking for them and moving in with friends or acquaintances is an option. Sometimes the mother is trying to disappear from a boyfriend or find a place that costs less. Home is a place that you live in for the moment, not the place that you were raised. This book is about those children who live at addresses that are common or non-descript, such as the house "Just Up the Road". May they be blessed to find a place of peace, order and normalcy in their lives.

꙳

Just Up The Road

Contents

Just Up The Road

Part 1

~

The Price of a Child

"My father told me once that the most important thing every man should know is what he would die for."
— *Tana French*

It was hot outside, and the lack of moving air in the old courthouse, left us sitting in a dim, stuffy Judge's chamber. His retirement was within the month and his approach to work was very casual. He didn't like to wear robes and kept his feet propped on the corner of the long brown table. He preferred the casual approach, as did the Prosecutor, who I would bet had never taken the time to read my court petition. I had been in court that day because of a mother who was emotionally abusive. Tom was a submissive man and his wife Carolyn lashed out at everyone. While visiting her home, I had watched her call her children, "little brats and liars" while they hunkered in corners. She considered them ungrateful after she had bought them expensive clothing and the 8 year old girl had manicures. A co-worker had been with me to their home and had also observed the disgust and anger this mother had towards them. She would pull the three year old to her chest, hold him tight saying what an angel he was and then with a face like the wicked witch of the west, blame the others for all of her problems. After all, she was a busy business woman and how dare they break her heart by talking to us, even if their father had scratches on his face, was sleeping in the truck, and name calling was occurring every day.

The Judge stared at me and asked, "If I called you a liar, would you feel berated?" He was referring to words used in my assessment referencing emotional abuse. They were not my words, but those that can be picked from a pick-list in order to describe what a worker observes. The words blaming and berated are identifiers of the legal definition of emotional abuse. This was my first time with this Judge and I was confused by his questioning. The Judge chuckled and the Prosecutor sat like a lump not speaking. In CPS court cases, the Prosecutor represents the State and is supposed to represent our position. It is very difficult for anyone to prove emotional or psychological abuse, and according to this Judge, I had failed to prove that screaming, blaming, name calling, and seeing your father hit is emotionally or psychologically abusive. My co-worker had gone to the extent of testifying by imitating her tone and yelling to describe what we had seen. The Judge asked us to leave and shortly thereafter we learned the case had been dismissed. I felt bad there was nothing we could do to help these children, but certainly we had not seen the last of this family. When there are problems in families, they can only stay hidden for so long before another incident occurs. There is an old expression that says "a whale always has to come up for air" and eventually, this family would reappear.

As I left the Judge's side chamber and walked out into the light of the secretary's office, others were talking about a news report which said a social worker from a different organization was missing. *Right From the Start* is a non-profit organization that works with high risk babies and their parents. Its purpose is to give babies a better start and is totally voluntary for families. While I had never met this person, we all share a common bond and a working knowledge of a world few know exists. We worry about each other and understand being alone and dealing with clients who are angry and aggressive.

According to the report, her absence had occurred the previous day and was just now becoming urgent and gaining media attention. Brenda Yeager was supposed to have had her last visit with a family in a remote area of our county and then returned home to her adjacent one. When she had not arrived, her husband had called a Supervisor and reported her missing. Together they were piecing together her schedule for the day and trying to figure out when she had last been seen and where her last visit would have been.

That day had started out on the wrong foot and it wasn't getting any better. Aggravated, worried and hungry, my co-workers and I walked down the courthouse steps for lunch. As always, we hoped we had not gotten a parking ticket because it would be five dollars more out of our small paycheck. It was pretty much impossible to leave court and put quarters in a meter, and so we got tickets just like everyone else. While it may seem trivial, it added to our frustration when we made so little and were also charged a fee to work in the city; a city whose potholes did a number on our cars.

In order for anyone to make sense of my ramblings, you need to know that just a few months before; I had been given a family to investigate named Foster-Forney. She had given birth to twin baby girls and they were staying at the Ronald McDonald House near the hospital. My first visit with the family had been at the Ronald McDonald house and I recall being pleasantly surprised at how nice the facilities were. The rooms were need based and free to families with loved ones that are hospitalized for serious conditions or needed long term care. Often they provided temporary housing for families living too far from the hospital. Stephen and Rosemary couldn't afford to go back and forth, even though they were fairly local, and so an exception was made.

This young couple had just had twin baby girls, and while one twin had been released and could be in the room with the parents, the other remained in the NICU and would need heart surgery. The hospital was concerned the parents were not making many visits to the sick twin and also wondered whether their housing would be adequate when they left. It was my job to make sure there wasn't any neglect occurring and to be certain their home was ready and livable when the babies were released.

I recall walking down the long carpeted hallway at the facility, finding their door number and waiting for Stephen to answer. The baby with them appeared to have just been changed and the mother who had been asleep was still groggy. In addition to their bed and bathroom, there was a crib for the baby, television, game system and other necessities for the family. Originally, this investigation had been assigned to another worker, but I had been told there was a personality conflict and so it was reassigned to me. Stephen told me off the bat that he didn't like people in his business and bothering them. I told him I understood and after some small talk, I put on my good ole girl face and tried to get him to understand I was there to help if possible. I leaned forward and tapped my file against his leg, while asking him to give me a chance. His response was firm and chilly; "Don't ever touch me again". I apologized, promised not to, and went on to ask a few questions. He told me that they were married, but later in the conversation, Rosemary gave me a different last name for herself. She was lower functioning and you could tell right away that Stephen was the one in control. His anger and behavior were paired with a suspicion of everyone, and yet I felt if I could get him to relax and trust me a little, we would be fine. I explained that I was there to make sure they were not accused of not visiting their baby and to make sure they had the things they needed when they went home. He said they didn't need anything other than to be left alone. I asked him why someone would say they had not been to visit their baby and his answer was that he didn't like watching the baby alone when Rosemary went to the hospital, and he didn't want to take the this baby back there. Stephen continued that if some of his family could come, they would go see the other baby girl more often. When I questioned Rosemary about their different last names, she told me they were not married. This immediately provoked an unexpected rage in Stephen and he shouted, "You are fucking everything up; you bitch". I wasn't sure if he was worried about not being allowed to stay at the Ronald McDonald house unmarried or if it had something to do with State benefits. Nevertheless, after that outburst, it was the least of my worries. My gut reaction had been to tell him that this was no way to speak to the woman that had just given birth to his children. I recall him becoming quiet, crossing his arms and slouching down in the corner chair.

Not wanting to lose any rapport, I quickly switched directions and commended them for wanting to be close for the baby and left them with a card and the know-ledge that I would be back to check on them. Visitation reports were faxed over from the hospital social work department and I continued to keep in contact concerning the other baby. After several weeks, the infant girl in the hospital was ready to have heart surgery, and even though she put up a good fight, she passed away. I couldn't imagine their grief. I called the family that day and expressed my sympathy, but also had to tell them that I would need to come out to their home soon and be sure they had everything they needed for their other baby girl. Again, Stephen was not happy, but agreed when I told him that it was necessary in order for me to get out of their lives. He gave me a number to call so I could leave a message and they could call me back.

They were my first appointment one hot summer day and I recall the long drive out winding, country roads. I had problems finding the house and needed to stop several times to ask for directions. Eventually, I drove through a metal cattle gate that said "Private Property". The lengthy dirt and grass road, opened to a block house that had a tar paper roof and cracks filled with orange, spray insulation from a can. The home was air-tight and other than lots of beer cans out front, it looked fine from the outside. Knocking, I waited and when there was no answer, I drove a little further to the end of road and saw the family cemetery. It appeared that the other baby girl had recently been buried there, but I didn't get out to be sure. Driving back to an area with phone service, I called Stephen and Rosemary and left another message. They returned my call and said they had forgotten about the visit and so we rescheduled again for the following week. I reasoned that at least it be easier finding their house the next time.

I looked forward to closing out this investigation and hoped everything was adequate. This relationship had lasted a long time and while I felt sad for the family, I certainly didn't want to be in their lives any longer than necessary. The following week, I drove the long grassy road again and walked to the door once more. Stephen opened it and welcomed me into their modest home. While there wasn't a lot of furniture, the baby was sleeping in her crib and Rosemary seemed happy and proud that things were clean and in order. I wished them well after seeing that their cabinets were full and that the electricity was on and running. The baby had stacks of diapers and cans of formula and I knew doctor appointments had already been scheduled. I left that day and entered my last contact into the computer. In my mind, I hoped the baby would have a good life. She had a lot of disadvantages ahead and it wouldn't be easy. I had no idea that the hospital had made arrangements with *Right from the Start* to make visits to their home.

The day after my court case, I glanced at the ten o'clock news before going to bed. It seemed that Brenda Yeager was a middle-aged woman that had worked for *Right from the Start* for a long time. She had been going to homes to make sure that babies were progressing developmentally and had diapers and food. Her family said it was not unusual for her to dip into her own pocket to make sure every family was well supplied. She loved her job and had been doing it for years. I stopped as the news report began and sat back down on the couch.

I was prepared for the reporter to say that Brenda had finally arrived home after being lost or having car problems. It so was easy to do when you traveled in unfamiliar territory and cell service was spotty at best. What I heard instead was that early in the evening, a burned-out car had been found after neighbors reported seeing smoke. The camera panned out showing a remote area, cattle gate, grass and dirt road. My mind raced to understand what was happening and how this all fit together. The reporter was saying that Brenda's last visit was with Stephen Foster, Jr. and Rosemary Forney. The car that had been found contained a burned body and police believed it to be the body of Brenda Yeager. I felt sick, lost control and began crying. The only thing I could think of was, "Why did they choose her and not me"? I called my Supervisor, who could give few words of comfort; this had never happened here before. Her advice was to take a few days off, but I knew if I did, I would never go back.

That night the couple was arrested and by morning had confessed they had turned up the music and Stephen had hid behind a blanket used as a curtain. At first he attempted to hit Brenda over the head with a pan in order to render her unconscious. When that hadn't worked, he had drug her in the bedroom at knife point and tried to smother her with a pillow. Rosemary had been ordered to help him with a plastic bag when Brenda had tried to fight. Stephen Foster Jr. later admitted to sexually assaulting Brenda and putting her body in the car that he had then set on fire. According to him, he needed help to do this and so he went and got his father to help him with gasoline.

Up until this point, false bravado and a fearless attitude had made me feel safe and assertive. I suddenly felt vulnerable and my false wall of protection had shattered. Part of me wanted to crawl under the covers and never come out, but I also realized that Brenda Yeager had tried to help this family and they must have saw her as a threat. The part that didn't make any sense was that I had been the threat. She was there to help them and not to take their baby away. If there would have been problems at the time, I would have asked for a Judge's order and had that child removed. I mourned for her and her family and this senseless killing. My days of ignoring angry clients and feeling invincible were gone forever.

A few days later, Lisa from economic services came to my desk to talk. She had heard I had previously worked with this family and she had been the Foster/Forney's economics service worker. She was troubled because as the search was on for Brenda, Rosemary had come into the office to renew her food stamp application. In addition, the Ronald McDonald House was upset because both a television and video gaming system were missing from the room in which they had stayed. We were both speechless at how any heart could be so callous and cold. Brenda Yeager gave her life and saved a child from a questionable future. We continued by believing that what we did somehow mattered.

For a short time, meetings were held to discuss new safety precautions and the public was somewhat surprised that as workers, we didn't go in pairs. It was hard enough as individuals to cover the investigations that came in and would have been impossible to have accomplished in pairs. There were self-defense classes offered, but I had no intentions of fighting with a client. For a while, there was also talk about radios that could be used to call in (if there was signal), and who would we radio without a dispatcher? All of these things cost money. There were meetings for suggestions and the police decided to move our requests for assistance to a higher priority level. For a while, Supervisors wanted us to religiously sign in and out, and while most of us were already doing this, it appeared to be a way to cover their asses more than to help us. We joked that it would help them find us after we were dead. In the end nothing changed, except for a law making it just as serious to kill a social worker, as to kill a police officer. As anyone can imagine, if we were already dead, this wouldn't help much and if someone would kill a police officer, they wouldn't think twice about us.

The following is an example of the sense of urgency that lasted for just a few months. This picture was in the local paper, showing a police vehicle driving the road to the Foster-Forney's house.

Social workers want more protection

Police investigate the discovery of a body believed to be that of missing social worker Brenda Yeager on Friday in southern Cabell County. The National Association of Social Workers has emphasized the need for better protection of social workers in response to Yeager's death.

Curtis Johnson/The Herald-Dispatch

August 03, 2008 @ 12:00 AM
LAURA WILCOX
The Herald-Dispatch

Better protection is needed for social workers in West Virginia, says the West Virginia chapter of the National Association of Social Workers. The chapter's executive director recently emphasized the need for improvements in response to the death of Brenda Lee Yeager, a social worker who went missing in the Mount Union area of Cabell County on Wednesday. Friday, West Virginia State Police, arrested Steven Anthony Foster Jr., 23, Rosemary

Forney, 22, and Steven Anthony Foster Sr., 51, in the death of Yeager. Foster Jr. and Forney are charged with murder and Foster Sr. is charged with third-degree arson, conspiracy and disposal of a body. First Sgt. A. L. Cummings of the West Virginia State Police said no new developments in the case were expected on Saturday."At this time, we're still putting all the pieces together," he said. Police reported that Yeager, of Hamlin, was making a scheduled home visit to 4293 Mount Union Road, where Foster Jr. and Forney lived with their infant. When troopers and deputies from the Cabell County Sheriff's Office arrived at the residence, they found a car and body on fire. Cummings said the infant was not at the home when police made the arrest."In my 31 years in social work, I don't think I've seen a crime this heinous perpetrated against a social worker in the line of duty," said Samuel A. Hickman, executive director of the West Virginia chapter of the National Association of Social Workers. Hickman said the job of a social worker takes courage and commitment and it can be just as dangerous as public safety work. Seventy percent of front-line child welfare workers have been victims of violence or threats while on the job, according to information from the American Federation of State, County and Municipal Employees. Hickman said awareness must increase in the profession and among lawmakers to make changes and put funding in place to protect social workers. The association wants to see policies and staff levels that insure social workers never go alone into potentially violent situations. The chapter also says social workers should have self-defense training and technology to insure their safety. Brenda would probably be alive today had she not called on this family alone, Hickman said.

Curtis Johnson/The Herald-Dispatch

A gate leads down a private drive where authorities said they found a woman's body Friday morning in southern Cabell County.

Police received information that led them to her body and a burned-out vehicle.
Woman admits killing social worker

Lori Wolfe/The Herald-Dispatch

Rosemary Forney pleaded guilty to first degree murder and kidnapping Tuesday morning in the July 30, 2008, death of social worker Brenda Lee Yeager.

February 16, 2010 @ 10:05 PM
CURTIS JOHNSON
The Herald-Dispatch

Rosemary Forney says fear that a social worker would take away her infant daughter motivated her and the child's father to kill. Forney, now 24, received two consecutive life sentences Tuesday after pleading guilty to kidnapping and first-degree murder in the July 30, 2008, death of Brenda Lee Yeager. Forney admitted to holding Yeager against her will and later using a garbage bag to suffocate the 51-year-old social worker after Yeager had come to her home. Cabell Circuit Judge Alfred Ferguson, who handed down the sentence, called it a classic case of first-degree murder, possibly the worst case heard during his more than 32 years on the bench. He used words such as "senseless," "violent," "premeditated" and "malicious." "It just should not have happened," he said. "This is a totally innocent victim. Sometimes people when they get shot, they are involved in something. But this girl, lady, was doing nothing wrong at all. She was just doing her job." Forney and Yeager first met at an area hospital, where her daughter's twin sibling had died. Yeager was assigned to help the family, which included Forney and live-in father Stephen Foster Jr. They set a date at the hospital for Yeager to check on the surviving child during a visit to the couple's home, located on Mount Union Road near the Cabell-Wayne county line. Foster and Forney did not have a working telephone. Therefore the parties never talked again, and the couple grew anxious. Forney said Tuesday the child's father had convinced her Yeager intended to take custody of the surviving child. That led them to decide the Hamlin, W.Va., resident must die, yet they never devised a plan until after she arrived. Investigators previously had testified that Yeager was hit in the head with a frying pan, held at knifepoint, sexually assaulted and suffocated at the couple's residence. The victim's body and vehicle later were burned to hide evidence, investigators said. Forney acknowledged the frying pan, kidnapping and suffocation at Tuesday's hearing. She confessed to her role without hesitation, apologized and sought forgiveness. She told the court she mistakenly thought she could get away with the crime. "I thought I would, but obviously I couldn't," she said. "I have too much guilt." The two consecutive life sentences, part of a plea agreement with prosecutors, came with no eligibility for parole until Forney serves 30 years behind bars. She gets credit for nearly 19 months of pre-trial incarceration. That will make her 52 at her first parole hearing. Jamie Jones spoke on behalf of Yeager's family, whose members shed tears during the hearing. He said Yeager, his mother-in-law, did not plan to take the child from the residence. Instead, her job included taking families bottles and diapers, along with providing other assistance. Her death prompted many calls for new state legislation to better protect social workers. Cabell County Prosecutor Chris Chiles and Jones equate the punishment to life sentence. The son-in-law called it the harshest punishment allowed by state law. He believed the case was more deserving of the death penalty, something prohibited in West Virginia for many years. "She doesn't deserve the breath she's still drawing," Jones said after court. "Until this state gets leaders with a backbone that are going to bring back a penalty that criminals will be afraid of, this is going to continue to happen. "You can pass all of the laws you want. It's just ink on paper," Jones added. Tuesday's guilty plea followed recent defeats for Forney's defense. It failed in January to win a change of venue for a trial, and lost arguments to toss out Forney's police confession in December. Chiles said Tuesday his side would have convinced jurors that Yeager was kidnapped by holding the social worker against her will to seek sexual gratification. Forney explained her role in the murder by saying she helped Foster hold the victim. They both participated in placing the garbage bag over Yeager's head, Forney said. "This is a terrible act," Chiles told the court. "We feel the penalties we agreed upon are appropriate." A jury conviction may have garnered a life sentence without parole, but the family hoped for quick closure in accepting the plea agreement. Jones said family members were cautious and actively involved in negotiations. They staunchly opposed an offer that would have secured the conviction without Forney's admission of guilt, a method often used by an attorney that keeps details of the crime and its motivation a mystery. He said family members found any such method unacceptable. They felt her admission would hold more weight with a parole board three decades from now. "Very much so," Jones said. "Her parole board, some of them haven't probably haven't been born yet." In exchange for Forney's admission, the prosecution agreed to dismiss counts of assault during the commission of a felony, second-degree sexual assault and concealment of a human body. Chiles said in April 2009 no plea offer would be considered for Forney or Foster, but Tuesday he said the ability to secure consecutive life sentences changed his mind. Foster is scheduled to appear in Ferguson's court for a pre-trial hearing Wednesday morning, Feb. 17th. Chiles said Tuesday no plea offer had been extended to Foster, but unlike in April 2009, the prosecutor did not close the door to such a possibility. There is no agreement for Forney to provide testimony at her co-defendants' trials, although Chiles said her right to protect herself from self-incrimination would no longer be a factor. Also charged with crimes linked to Yeager's death is Foster's father, Stephen Foster Sr. He faces allegations of felony third-degree arson, concealment of a human body and accessory after the fact to murder. Plea negotiations with the elder Foster had broken down in June 2009, according to in-court comments Chiles made to Ferguson at the time, "I deserve a lot worse".

Crystal Daniels Weible

Stephen Foster Jr. entered a guilty plea Thursday, April 1, 2010, to killing, kidnapping and hiding the body of a social worker Brenda Yeager.

April 02, 2010 @ 12:00 AM
CURTIS JOHNSON
The Herald-Dispatch

Stephen Foster Jr. received consecutive sentences of life in prison with mercy for suffocating, kidnapping, sexually assaulting and hiding the body of a beloved social worker from Lincoln County in late July 2008. Both Foster and the victim's son, Joshua Yeager, agreed the punishment wasn't severe enough for killing a woman who visited Foster's home only to care for the defendant's infant daughter after the baby's twin had died. "I deserve a lot worse than this," Foster said. Joshua Yeager told the court his spoken words showed restraint for a man

~ 31 ~

who gave no mercy to his mother, Brenda Lee Yeager. Before her death, she was in the prime of her life feeling the best she had since high school, he said. "In my opinion, you should spend the rest of your life being beaten, sodomized, molested and tortured," he told Foster. "When you die you can burn in Hell for all eternity. I believe in the death penalty, but death is too good for you." Yeager, 51, of West Hamlin, W.Va., died July 30, 2008, at the home of Foster and co-defendant Rosemary Forney. Yeager had traveled to the couple's residence to see their infant daughter, to whom she had been assigned to assist in providing care. West Virginia State Police found her body and vehicle two days later, both burned, in an area near the couple's house at 4293 Mount Union Road near the Cabell-Wayne county line. Foster confessed to first-degree murder, kidnapping and concealing a human body, saying he killed Yeager in fear she planned to take custody of his daughter. He entered a no contest plea to second-degree sexual assault. "I went too far," he said. "I did something really bad." Circuit Judge Dan O'Hanlon accepted Foster's pleas and ordered the agreed-upon punishment, but the judge said Foster's reasoning provided no justification for murder and sexual assault. He called the act "absolutely unbelievable" to have been done "to someone as good as this woman." "Any attempt to justify what you did is nothing but garbage," O'Hanlon said. "You deserve everything you're getting and more. If I could give you more, I would." Foster openly confessed to burning Foster's body, but the prosecution dismissed counts of third-degree arson and assault during the commission of a felony as part of the plea agreement. Prosecutor Chris Chiles, who a year ago vowed no plea offer would be considered for Foster or Forney, called the agreement a good plea as it secured consecutive life sentences. Trial had been set for May 12. "This is a crime that cries out for a harsh penalty," Chiles told the court. "With this plea, we're able to do that with-out putting the family through hearing all of the testimony." Joshua Yeager spoke moments after his sister Julie Prichard. They joined another of the victim's children, her sister and her co-workers at Thursday's plea and sentencing hearing. Prichard blamed Foster for taking her mother's life "with his bare hands." She said he killed a woman whose only aim was to provide assistance, such as food, clothing and diapers. "She helped everybody," Prichard said. "She did in my court," O'Hanlon recalled on a personal note. "She only cared about people. She was a wonderful, wonderful person." Prichard said her mother never planned to take the couple's infant. She said they should have simply refused the service, instead of opting to kill and leave her loved ones with nothing but memories. "All we have are pictures, including those of this horror story," Prichard said. "The first thing I see in the morning is her house, and it's the last thing I see when I lock my doors at night." Per the attorneys' agreement, the first-degree murder and kidnapping convictions carry consecutive sentences of life with mercy. The sexual assault punishment means an additional 10 to 25 years in prison. The concealment penalty will run together with the other punishments. That means Foster must serve at least 40 years before he is eligible for parole consideration, although no such release is guaranteed. He received it for 20 months of pre-trial incarceration. That means he will be 63 at his first parole hearing.

Part 2

◞

In the Beginning

*"But often life asks much of you, and you either honor
life by answering with all your heart, or you cower
your way into your grave."*   *— James Clemens*

Just Up The Road

It was my first two weeks out of training with Child Protective Services and I definitely didn't know what I'd gotten myself into. Outside the trees were orange and gold, the kind of day that warms your body and smells of dry leaves and earth. I was shadowing another worker, as we walked into the cool, green PICU to talk with a little boy with burns. The State Police, medical staff and Assistant Prosecutor were waiting to find out how he had gotten the horrific marks on his stomach and back and it was a CPS workers job to interview him. The small room was crowded with machines and a seemingly large bed held the body of a very small little boy named Jeremy. Jamie handed me her pad of paper and asked me to write down his words while she asked questions. The Trooper, who came in the room, was the only person the child was interested in and Jeremy was fascinated with his hat and gun. It became obvious that he would be the one to build the rapport and answer the ultimate question of who had done this. Jeremy could have cared less about us and continued coloring in a book the nurses had given him.

Trooper Pruitt started coloring a picture on a different page and Jeremy wanted to see what he was drawing. As he drew a picture of his hat, he told Jeremy that he would show it to him, if he would tell him what happened to him. It took patience and time, but slowly Jeremy nodded and quietly murmured that his foster mother had held him in hot water and he's wasn't supposed to tell. Jamie and I walked past the smiling woman in the lobby and got on the elevator in silence. We rode back to the office without a word and while Jamie sat on the picnic table behind the building, I went to my cubicle to process what had just happened.

While she had been fostering siblings, a boy and a girl, the boy often complained about not having any toys and his sister had everything. This was explained away as sibling rivalry by the foster mother. When the assigned worker went to get the little girl out of the home, she took pictures of the rooms. Sitting at her desk, she flipped through them and saw a little girl's room filled with toys and clothes and a little boy's room that was almost bare. It was a moment of truth and a real eye-opener. We had taken the foster mother's word for things and hadn't really looked carefully at the bedrooms. Because of the extensive training a foster parent has to go through, no one expects such horrific mistakes can occur, but they do. Jeremy's foster mother was later charged with child abuse and would never again be a foster parent or be able to legally care for anyone's children. Hopefully, as the visible scars healed on Jeremy, the emotional ones would also.

Driving home that day, I felt certain that taking this job had been a huge mistake and if my parents had any idea of what I had just seen, they would help me until I could find another job. After my divorce, in addition to part-time jobs and student loans, my parents had supported me until I could find a full-time job. That day my mother listened and then told me to go back to work. Her words were essentially that "I had been raised tougher than that". I felt naïve and thrown into a world that few know exists. Five years has passed and my innocence is gone. I have been changed in ways that I may never fully understand. It's a sad feeling, both for me, and for the children I encountered.

Part 3

~

Dirty Houses

"My idea of housework is to sweep the room with a glance."

-Erma Bombeck

Time passed and fall had turned into a cold, damp winter. I was given a report of a filthy house, children with lice for over a year and a home that wasn't habitable. Sometimes this was the truth and other times, the family has merely made an enemy that saw Child Protective Services as sweet revenge. We didn't usually make appointments on our first visit because we wanted to see the family in their everyday environment.

I hopped over the muddy, leaf-filled water at the curb, and walked up the steps to the door of an old brick located in an older area of town. Melissa, the children's mother, led me through blankets used to divide rooms and keep in the heat. After the first two heavy blankets, my feet began sliding in dog feces that covered the rough wooden floors. Two half-dressed little children ran past barefoot and into another room. This was the city and I was informed by the children that they had bunnies and chickens in the basement. As I walked into the kitchen, I discovered that the walls were not black as first thought, but covered in roaches. The trash piles had drawn gnats and a strong sour smell permeated the air; it was a smell all social workers knew, but couldn't adequately describe.

I stepped carefully back into the living room and sat lightly on the edge of a well-worn chair. I needed to get services started with the Anderson's and so I asked Melissa if she would turn on a lamp so I could see to write. The heat from the lamp drew the roaches and they were falling everywhere. I would occasionally stop writing and flick one off my paper or myself. The mother had attempted to treat the lice with Vaseline, but it wasn't working; both girls had hair stuck to the sides of their head. The little boy had been given a crew-cut and was fine except for his feet. These children had missed a lot of school and this home wasn't healthy. After writing down some agreed upon services, I stepped over more dog feces and circled up the steps to the second floor. The bedrooms were bare except for the dirty mattresses and matching brown pillows. I recall thinking that it wasn't any wonder that the lice were alive and well as I cautiously walked back down the steps.

Melissa promised to call an exterminator that day, to have the floors clean and bleached and to treat and comb out the children's hair by the end of the day. The dogs were going to be crated and we discussed the need for clean bedding. In other words, the brown colored pillows needed to be thrown out. Most families are not this agreeable to change and possibly they were just relieved the children could stay. Nevertheless, five hours later they had accomplished what was expected and necessary.

Unfortunately, instead of having the nits removed, the mother had given both girls crew cuts. I felt bad for them but knew this mother was at least motivated. This family would need life skill services and additional parenting in their home to keep it from getting this bad again. These children needed to be in school and to experience the feeling of cleanliness most children take for granted.

When I returned the following week, I decided to ask about the chickens and rabbits and if they had been removed from the basement. The father told me they were taken care of and were "in the freezer". Somewhat speechless, I recognized that at least there would be food to eat in the months ahead. This story had a happy ending…unless of course you were a chicken or rabbit.

ᴧ

Hoarders

Dirty houses are quite different than those owned by hoarders. Hoarders are people that are attached to their dirt and don't want to let go of it. One particular home stood out because teachers had been putting up with the odor of three young girls for quite a while. Their concern had prompted them to go the extra mile and drive past the home to check it out. What they saw outside convinced them to make a call to our office and I was the lucky winner.

The Tanner's had been renting a small dilapidated house at the base of a hill, for several years. The porch and yard were piled high with the rusted out skeletal remains of unidentified items mixed with boxes. Sometimes the outside of a home can look this way and then the inside will be acceptable. That day I drove down the hill, looked for the address and prayed that the one with the garbage wasn't the one I needed. I parked in the narrow turn and took a deep breath as I realized that the worst house on the street was waiting for me. The old school papers lying on the steps led to an enclosed porch piled high with boxes, mattresses and dirty clothing. Squeezing in between the piles, I found just enough room to knock on the door. Through the door, I heard a woman yell that I couldn't come in the house. While still talking through the door, I explained to her who I was and that I really needed to talk with her. The door cracked open an inch and it was all I needed to see. Glenna was standing four feet higher than me on top of paper and garbage and I soon realized when she said I couldn't come in, it had nothing to do with being welcome. Together she pulled while I pushed and I joined her on top of the layers. That day I was certain I had found the dirtiest and most cluttered home in the State. All of the rooms were in the same condition, the kitchen blocked with garbage, dishes with old food, and both the oven and a space heater were being used for heat. It was frightening to see so much trash that close to an open oven.

By far the most disgusting room was the bathroom which had smeared feces all over the walls and used toilet paper stuck on the floor and piled almost to the ceiling. Trying to be polite, I asked if there was a problem with the toilet and

Glenna said that they were just afraid to flush it and had began using the tub as a toilet. I asked her how long it had been since they had flushed the toilet and her answer was seven years. Seven years!!! That was when they had first moved there. Her explanation was that they had previously lived in a trailer, and every time they flushed, it would clog. Now, they didn't bother. The odor of old rotten food, garbage and fecal matter was indescribable. In addition, there were feral cats sheltering under the house and so the smell of cat urine came up through the floor and garbage. The girls didn't have beds to sleep in, even though the unassembled wood bunks leaned against the wall. The youngest child had been sleeping in an old chair that was leaning over on a pile. This situation was one in which a protection plan needed to be completed and the children placed with family members until the home could improve. I knew that it could easily be condemned by the health department, but then what? Together we arranged for a special garbage pickup each week and they promised to eliminate at least twenty bags per day. In addition, the girls were allowed to return during the day to help clean their room and paint. While painting was not a primary concern, it was important to the girls to make their room special and they were excited.

Behind every home of a hoarder is a story and this home wasn't any different. Glenna appeared depressed and hadn't left the home in some time. Surprisingly, the father looked like a homeless person, and yet worked for a company that hauled hazardous waste—Yes, I saw the irony. He was very open man and told me he had an associate's degree in computers. When I asked about his childhood and what his worst memory was, he described living with his parents until a house fire. Afterwards, he had been sent to live with his grandparents and had slept every night in his clothes, with all his belongings in his pockets. He feared another fire and wanted to be able to run and not lose anything. I asked if he thought that this memory had anything to do with keeping everything and his reply was "hadn't thought about it, but probably". I wish I was able to say that this story had a happy ending, however, even with a case manager in the home every week, not much more was accomplished. Unless someone is willing or forced to change, it just doesn't occur. Because the children were older, once the main safety issues were removed, State law required that we remove ourselves from their lives. For the time being, the floors were clear except for the parent's bedroom where much of the stuff had been relocated. They could cook in the kitchen, use the bathroom and the girls had beds to sleep in for now.

*

Cows, Dogs and Chickens

Every worker had an animal encounter story which was hilarious, scary, or just plain weird. I've laughed at a worker being chased by a bull, a chicken that flapped into someone's hair, or a worker tapping on a cardboard window and having a large dog come barreling through. Fortunately for Brian, he was only pushed down and had a good face licking.

Experience taught us to always shake a fence before opening a gate, to keep an eye out for a dog bowl, toy, or a grassless patch with a chain. If a dog was around the corner on a chain, you needed to decide how long that chain was and whether it would still reach you. Some workers carried bones with them, but I was never sure how fast a dog might eat, or if I would look better than the bone. Just because someone had a great relationship with their pet, didn't mean they would like me...unless of course it was for dinner. On the other hand, I have had a pit bull sneak up and lay it's head on my lap. I've also had a client hold a bedroom door while six pits tried to have me for a meal. Chows and German Sheppard's are very protective and will pretend to like you until you come near their people.

When it comes to the most unusual, it was surprising to see an alligator in a tank of a small apartment. I have no idea why anyone would want an alligator with children around, but they did. Early in training, I had tagged along with another worker to a two-story white house which supposedly had twenty-three rats. There were concerns that the children could be bitten and in my mind I envisioned giant rodents crawling all around the house. It was not a place I was looking forward to seeing. An irritated woman answered the door and wanted to know who we were, why we were there, and she wanted to know immediately. Training had taught us to gather information first and then talk about the problem. When an individual is angry, they are less likely to answer the questions needed for an assessment. In other situations, it's best to address the issue quickly to alleviate the stress.

My co-worker immediately asked the woman if she had twenty-three rats in the home and she emphatically said, "NO" and then blurted, "I only have eighteen". I'm afraid I couldn't help but laugh a little at that answer. Thankfully they were all in a cage, and while they were gross to look at crawling all over each other, there was no way they could get out. Sometimes the very people that abuse their children take great care of their animals. Other times, those that are abusive to animals, treat their children the same.

My favorite animal story began with a report that a little boy named Mark had told his teacher his home didn't have any water. It was a cold and rainy day outside; the kind of day that makes it hard to drive up hills that are nothing but ruts filled with muddy water. When I found the green trailer at the end of the wet clay road, it was leaning on the side of a mountain.

I attempted to avoid the tire tracks filled with water and mud and tried to find something to step on that didn't stick to my shoes. Trekking towards the trailer on tiptoes and hopping from side to side, I made it without too much buildup on my shoes. Once there, I hung onto the wooden railing and pulled myself up on the deck leading to the back door. I fully expected the condition inside to be equally soiled, but much to my surprise, the home was clean and neat. Mark's mom was gracious and showed me she had plenty of food, bottled water and that Mark had a bed.

Shortly after coming back into the living room, I explained to Angie that someone was concerned that she didn't have any water and had called us. While many people may not be able to pay their bill, Angie told me that a cow had fallen into their septic tank and so the water needed to be off while they worked on it. In the mountains, families will sometimes have a plastic tank slightly under ground for sewage treatment. Evidently, a cow had accidently stepped on top of the tank and it had collapsed from the cow's weight. Curiosity got the best of me and so I asked how they had gotten the cow out. Very matter-of-factly she said, "Tow truck". Surprised and taken aback, I asked, "What did you do with the cow?" Angie promptly said, "That's how we got all the meat in the freezer".

As it turned out, the water would be back on soon and the family would have beef for the winter. I returned to the office and told my Supervisor that the family had added carrots and potatoes to the tank, struck a fire underneath and was making stew for the winter. She laughed, but we both knew it was considered making the most of what you had; normal life for those that live in the mountains

Just Up The Road

Part 4

~

Secrets

"Children's bodies aren't like automobiles with the assailant's fingerprints lingering on the wheel. The world of sexual abuse is quintessentially secret. It is the perfect crime".

-Beatrix Campbell

Just Up The Road

As winter began and the cold sat in, we would receive calls concerning a lack of food or heat. When the electricity goes off, the food goes bad and old homes became cold quickly. My first winter call consisted of a little boy reporting to his teacher that he and his sister were living with their dad and it was cold. They were not supposed to tell or they would get in trouble. The father did not want me to come in because according to him, it was too messy. I explained this was not a problem and I needed to see him. While I had on a black wool pea coat, my fingers were still freezing in this home, so much so that I couldn't hold a pen to write. The children were not wearing coats and their noses were running. Both seemed excited to see me and while I was talking to their father, the little girl drew a picture and handed it to me. The picture was of a house and she had written the words, "I love you" underneath. There was something not quite right about this situation and yet, I couldn't quite put my finger on it.

The mother had recently left and was setting up her own residence. She knew these children were going to their father's after school. Additionally, men typically didn't like women telling them to what to do and tended to keep their distance. John sat close to me and kept calling me "dear", even as I tried to talk to him about his housing problems. After calling him "Sir" several times, he stopped. I became so cold that I couldn't finish the interview and told him that the children couldn't spend the night or return until the electric was turned back on. I took his disconnect slip to see if the Department could help with the bill and the mother arrived for the two young children. When Mary arrived, she said she had been picking them up every day and wasn't aware that there wasn't heat or food. She was very angry with John and this inability to provide for the family seemed to be the cause for their pending divorce. She had picked up their four year old son from preschool and Sarah, a fifteen year old step-daughter, was also in the car. She came in to pick up a few things and glanced at John out of the corner of her eye. He lifted one hand in a wave, but she ignored him and continued out the door.

While I had been looking into the housing needs of the family, I got a new report. The stepdaughter, who no longer had to go to her stepfather's, had told a counselor that she had been raped from the time she was six by this man. While the mother had been at work, he would bribe the child with computer time or telephone time in order to sleep with her. Benadryl had been given to the younger children to put them to sleep and keep them sleep. At times the step-daughter had even been told to give them the Benadryl. This had been going on for almost ten years and the reason for the creepy feeling was obvious.

It wasn't necessary for the State Police to give John a polygraph; he voluntarily confessed and didn't under-stand what the problem was if his step-daughter had been willing. We can only wonder how someone ends up with such a twisted sense of morality. He is now in prison and this young woman will have to grow up and learn to trust again.

The following appeared in the paper. Due to the nature of this story and others, the offender's names have been deleted. This is not to protect the abuser, but to protect the victims. News reports rarely know the family behind the police reports and that information is confidential. Hopefully these young victims will grow up and begin to heal; they don't need to be reminded.

Local man sentenced to 25 years for sex crimes

March 20, 2010 @ 12:00 AM
CURTIS JOHNSON
The Herald-Dispatch

A *************** man learned this week he will spend at least 25 years in prison, after being charged with a decade of sexual assault and abuse. ******************, 43, was sentenced Tuesday in Cabell Circuit Court, according to court documents. Judge Alfred Ferguson ordered a 15- to 35-year prison sentence for first-degree sexual assault and a 10- to 20-year sentence for sexual abuse by a parent, guardian or custodian. The punishments will be served one after the other. ********** had pled guilty in July 2009 to single counts of both crimes. The charges were included within a 20-count indictment that charged ********** with incidents from 1999 to 2008. It alleged 10 counts of sexual assault and as many counts of sexual abuse. Prosecutors agreed to dismiss 18 counts of the indictment in return for ********** admission. ********** has been incarcerated at the Western Regional Jail ever since his arrest in December of 2008. Criminal complaints at that time alleged the defendant used psychological intimidation and threats to coerce the victim. *********** must serve twenty-five years of the prison sentence before he is eligible for parole consideration. He could discharge the sentence in 27 and half years with good behavior. In addition to the prison sentence, ********** punishment also includes 25 years of supervised release and a mandatory, lifetime listing on the state's sex offender registry. He will receive credit for time served behind bars prior to this week's sentencing.

*

Bizarre and Fantastic Reports

It's difficult to comprehend what sex is from a child's perspective, especially if they have been told this is a game, or if the child believes this occurs in all families. This is especially true with very young children, and as a sexual abuse interviewer, I became familiar with what is called "bizarre and fantastic reports". Years ago, when a child said someone had touched them and then added "my cat killed him", it was dismissed as a child's imagination and would not stand up in court. Sometimes it was simply agreed upon that the child may have been referring to having bathroom help and it was dropped. Research has come to show that when a child says, "after that I flew away" or "I stabbed him with a knife", it is their way of getting away or protecting themselves from a terrible situation in which they have no control.

One summer, I was asked by another county to interview a little girl that had went there to visit her mother and her new boyfriend. Jessica was 4 years old and told me that mom's new friend Adam watched her at night, while her mother went to work. She said he would put her to bed and sometimes would lay down with her. This might not have been unusual, except for the fact that Jessica added, "my cat turned into a lion and came and bit him and made him leave". One time her dog had killed him and yet in real life, Adam was still very much alive. With new training, I knew to ask Jessica if this was "real, pretend, or what she had wished would have happened?" Jessica was adamant that she "wished it would have happened, because he touched her and it hurt". Thankfully, we had been taught to not stop when the cat turned into a lion or the child grew wings and flew away. This mother was protective, believed her child and Adam was arrested for child molestation. Sometimes the smallest bits of information can make the biggest difference.

Skin

The skin of children and adults can often tell us what has occurred in their lives. Social workers see their share of scabies, ringworm, lice and other conditions that may come from a less than clean environment. Many sexual abuse allegations have been substantiated because a child has a disease or rash which can only be obtained from sexual contact.

While others had heard of molluscum contagiosum, this doctor's report was something new for me and the pictures were disgusting. The ugly, mushroom shaped rash on Joey could have been spread through close sexual contact, or from the towel or hands of an infected individual.

The alleged perpetrator was a co-owner of a children's play place and Joey's mother had worked there for years. Allison trusted both the owner, Howard and his business partner Al, and so she often let Joey play while she worked in the office. According to Allison, she had experienced car problems and had called Howard and asked him to pick Joey up from daycare and keep him until she got there. When she was finally able to get back, Joey wasn't there. Al had told Howard that he was supposed to watch Joey and so he had taken him to his house. Howard had assumed there had been a change of plans and wasn't concerned. Allison was confused because she had never talked with Al. She also knew Joey didn't particularly like Al, especially when Al wanted to hold him. Even so, Allison set it aside for the time being, as a misunderstanding.

Weeks later, when Joey had a rash on his genital area, she took him to the doctor. She was told that he had molluscum contagiosum and was given an antibiotic. Joey told the doctor that Al had "bumps" too and this suddenly became alarming to everyone. She went to the police and they requested that a forensic interview be done by CPS. I tried talking with Joey to find out where he had seen the rash or if he had been touched, but Joey only wanted to show me his own itchy rash.

Essentially, I couldn't get any information from Joey and of course Al was denying anything had happened. I relayed this to the State Trooper and when she found out this rash could also be spread from child to child or from towels, she didn't feel she had enough evidence. Al told her he didn't have the rash and refused to provide any other information. While I felt we had enough for a polygraph based on Al taking Joey to his home, she disagreed, and we were left with nothing further to go on. I cringed when I thought of other children being around this man and being dropped off for parties. Fortunately, Howard took it seriously and decided to have Al do the books and not have contact with the children. While I thought this was a positive move, it also made it appear that Howard had some concerns about Al also. Thankfully, the last time I drove by the place, it was no longer in business.

*

The Sex Talk

If there is message that parents should have about sexual abuse, it is this... "Believe your child!!!" Trust that a child may have a pretend friend, but never a pretend toucher. No man or woman is worth the life or safety of your child. The number of parents that call their child a liar, or come up with another excuse for what has been reported, is way too many. Either they do not want to accept they could have been fooled, or that the person going to bed with them, could possibly be interested in their child. What they don't realize is that single parents are prime targets for child molesters and pedophiles. They can be so stressed from trying to work and be a parent that it is a huge relief when someone comes into their lives and wants to help out. This individual is affectionate, plays, tickles, buys toys, helps around the house, and at first the child really likes all of the attention.

The changes that have occurred in our culture now mean that grandparents no longer live in the home or just next door. The neighbors that once were family are no longer in the majority. Not only does a new boyfriend or step-parent bring themselves to the home, they bring extended family members that the birth parent doesn't know very well. Does this mean we can't trust anyone? No, it means that anyone that is around your child should be checked out by you and any discomfort you feel shouldn't be dismissed. Trust your instincts and if there is any doubt, this person must not be around your child. Do not bring people you have recently met around your children. Parents would never drop their children off at a daycare provided by sex offenders, however, when a parent leaves their child with a stranger or new friend, they are taking similar risks. State police sites, FBI sites, and internet sites such as "Family Watch Dog", are all excellent for doing research, but you are your child's guardian. Some people have been able to stay under the radar. Talk to their girlfriends, boyfriends, or other friends. Facebook or Google their names for any information you can find and don't assume what you are being told is right until you prove it. Find out if this person has a job, criminal history, substance abuse history, moves a lot, or has family? What does this person's family say about them or do they even have a familial relationship? These are all important questions to ask and no, you aren't being too protective.

Having said all of that, even the most protective parent, can still have this nightmare occur in their lives. Be sure your child feels comfortable talking to you and make sure they know they can trust you to protect them. If they are a victim whose trust has been violated, they will need your strength to be healthy again. Promise them that you will believe them and then do it!

Sexual abuse is very important to me because it has always been one area in which the offender doesn't get a second chance; they get incarcerated. We will not be offering services to anyone but the victim. The individual that abuses children will be going away. Empowering children is a wonderful feeling and truly humbling. I will always be thankful for the children that trusted me and allowed me to be their voice.

Just Up The Road

Part 5

~

Slow Parenting

*"Indifference and neglect often do more damage
than outright dislike."*   -
J.K. Rowling

Just Up The Road

Because of my experience with Stephen and Rosemary, I learned to be more cautious and so when I met Larry, I recognized the same personality traits right away. He was low-functioning, paranoid and aggressive. His wife, Lisa, was even more low-functioning and followed him both physically and emotionally. He didn't like the fact that I had came to his home to see if he had food and bedding, and he especially didn't like me moving the sheets he had up to certain rooms. Larry emphasized if I woke up the youngest, he would be "very, very angry". I took this as a threat and stopped. The three year old little girl didn't speak, had a black eye and each parent had a different story of how she had gotten hurt. Their eighteen month old daughter didn't walk, talk, or pull-up, and it was obvious if these children were going to progress, they needed more than what their parents could give them. I watched as the mother took a hamburger patty from a McDonald's bun and threw it on the dirty carpet for the baby. She couldn't grab it and so it laid there. I needed to discuss this family with my Supervisor and return as soon as possible.

When I came back for my second visit, my Supervisor had recommended a lot of services and I was there to tell them that they would be having people coming to their home each week to work with the girls. This time I had decided to bring a male co-worker with me and put pepper spray in my pocket; I wasn't taking chances. As I we got out of the car, Larry started to open the door and then quickly closed it when he saw my co-worker. When he opened it again, he was whispering to Lisa and this wasn't feeling right. This couple was illiterate and so I made sure that I explained everything in detail and why the girls needed help to grow and progress. My explanations only drew blank stares and agitation.

Within minutes, Larry left the living room, walked around the corner and out of sight. I turned to Tom and said, "If he comes back with a gun, we just need to talk fast and get out". Larry walked past and continued out the front door. As Lisa started to follow him, I asked her what was going on and could she stay and talk without her husband. She stopped moving and when Larry came back in, I wasn't sure what to expect. I can only assume that pacing helped him to think. He sat down and said that we could leave; his family didn't need anything because everyone in his family was late to begin walking and talking. He saw their delays as normal development. In reality, the delays were generational and changes would only come about through intensive treatment, therapy and lots of hope. Once again I explained if he didn't agree, I would have to contact the prosecutor and so it would be best if he agreed with the services. Larry took the papers, went to the dining room table and made an "X" next to what I had written.

Over the following months, the family refused to let providers of services inside and didn't answer the door. Numerous times they would lock their fence so that no one could enter. The 3 year old was found in the street many times and the police would find the mother asleep. A very determined case manager jumped the fence, only to be locked out. This was a perfect example of someone "not being compliant with services" and it meant we would be going to court to talk with a Judge.

While it is sad that some individuals aren't able to comprehend simple child care, it is more important to give children a chance to develop and have a normal life. Terminating parental rights is not an easy thing. Families are given many opportunities to change and to learn new or missing skills. These low-functioning parents eventually made it in front of a Judge who gave the girls a chance for a future. I watched the parents walk out of the courthouse alone and I still didn't believe they understood what had occurred. After they had refused to comply with a Judge's orders and work with services to help their children, taking the children was our only choice.

Visions

Combine genetics with environmental stressors such as little or no income, depression and lack of family support, and the increase in mental health problems becomes more prevalent. These conditions are often masked by drug use, or other self-medicating behaviors. No case is more unusual than my experience with Lisa and her girlfriend, Sara. I was first introduced to them when Lisa had a baby boy at the hospital. I happened to be there seeing another family, when one of the hospital social workers asked me to talk to a new mother;

the new mother was Lisa. When I walked into the room, she was holding the baby and Sara, her partner, was sitting in a chair reading the Bible. I congratulated her on the birth of her son and asked if the father had been to see him. Lisa explained that the father was a homeless veteran that she had slept with for a "dime bag" nine months ago. She knew his first name was Henry, and only had a general idea of where he might be located.

After gathering a little information, I explained to Lisa that the staff had some concerns that the baby was going through withdrawal. She was adamant that she had not used any drugs and asked if smoking cigarettes could be the reason. This was not the case and I explained that in order to help the baby, it would be best if she were honest. All the same, she refused to admit to anything and it was too late for testing. Because Lisa had come to the ER bleeding, and without prenatal care, there weren't any drug screens. By the time the infant showed signs of withdrawal, it was too late to test umbilical cord blood or meconium (the first bowel movement).

As I gathered history from Lisa, I realized this was either the most outrageous story ever told or the most horrific nightmare anyone could have endured. She said she had been raped by her father and become pregnant when she was just 10 years of age. According to Lisa, her parents had hid her in the house and when it was time for the baby to be born; her mother had tied her to her bed and left her alone. Lisa went on to say that after the birth, her father started a fire in the backyard barrel, and she was made to watch as he threw the baby in the fire. This had been her first pregnancy. Her second occurred after she had become an adult and had run away from home. She said she had been living under a bridge and began having terrible stomach pains. When she gave birth to a baby in the dead of winter, a man had let her live in his tent rather than outside. She explained how she had wrapped the baby in blankets to keep it warm and then later someone told her that he had died after she left the tent. According to her, other homeless people had buried the baby under the bridge, and for a while she thought maybe he had even been kidnapped. I asked her if she thought we should notify the police in order to find the baby's body, but according to her, she had already tried and he had either washed down the river, or they had lied. When I asked why she hadn't attempted to get someone to call an ambulance for her, she said it was snowing too hard. Lisa had an answer for every question and Sara was silent. According to her, no one else knew about these pregnancies.

As if it couldn't become more bizarre, Lisa told me she had been born with both male and female body parts and her mother had decided she would be a girl. Her exact words were, "The doctors had made her a girl". Lisa's mannerisms were more male than female and her hair was cut shorter than some men. I made a mental note to see if the Dr. had been able to tell whether Lisa had given birth before and if her genitalia were unusual in any way. Her partner Sara continued to sit quietly and read, as Lisa told me she had gotten an apartment and baby equipment with her disability check. She stated she loved her baby and wanted to be a good mother and I was more confused than ever. Could any of this really be true? I had read of terrible cases of abuse before and wondered if this was indeed possible? Her answers were swift and certain; I definitely needed additional information and my investigative abilities would be put to the test.

Before I left, Lisa told me her mother was coming to see the baby that evening. More confused, I asked her why she would let someone who had helped kill her first child be near this baby? She attempted to reassure me that she would watch her and make sure everything was okay, but I didn't feel good about this. She agreed that any visitors could be supervised by a nurse or social worker and I went back to the office.

Every once in a while, you tell your Supervisor a story and even they are astounded. This was definitely one of those times. At home that night, I got on Facebook and decided to see if Lisa or Sara had a webpage. I held my breath as their combined page came into view and I read what Sara had written. Her post proclaimed she was "A Goddess" and "to ask her any question and she had the answer". Suddenly, I knew I had failed to look at Sara and her own mental health problems. When I talked with Sara the next day, she told me that she had just been to see her mother and gave me her number as a reference. When I called her, she said she had not seen Sara in years and Sara had said it had only been months. She didn't have a job or any means of support and lacked any attachment to Lisa's baby. Lisa's family voiced concerns that Sara was only using her for a place to live and a means of support. Within a short time, this became obvious to everyone involved. Months passed without Sara making any attempt to get a job or to help out in any way.

The day following my first visit, the nursing staff had more concerns. While the baby had been with Lisa during the night, his diaper had not been changed. Furthermore, they couldn't get Lisa to wake up and take care of him. When they confronted her about this, she said she was too tired and needed her sleep. According to Lisa, Sara had gone out and gotten her a pill so she could get some sleep.

Within days, I received a call from a service provider, who said that Sara, (the Goddess) had professed this baby was to be born on Halloween. I quickly looked through the information and sure enough, Lisa had given birth on Halloween. Did presenting with bleeding mean she had tried to put herself into labor in order for it to be a Halloween birth? The thought was disturbing and once again, I needed more information.

After a signed release from Lisa, the hospital social work department was able to provide me with Lisa's medical history. In the last 2 years, Lisa had come to the ER at least twice a month with a wide range of problems. The list of complaints included having been raped, broken beer bottles inside of her, cuts on her wrists, and minor fights and bruises, all totaled more than 48 visits.

As I sat in the hospital conference room, going over this with the social worker, a nurse knocked and said she had just overheard Sara say to Lisa, "This place is just like Auschwitz, we might as well put him in the oven now!" I asked the nurse if she had documented this and if she would be willing to testify in court. Her answer was "yes" and we finally had enough to get a verbal order from a Judge and could take custody of the baby. Lisa would need psychiatric help and a better evaluation than the hospital was able to provide. After her first court appearance, she was given an improvement period and occasionally I would see her when she came to visit her son at the department. The Judge dismissed Sara as having any part in the case and a court worker found the elderly man whom Lisa said was the father. He was indeed homeless.

Her Aunt told me she had pictures of every year Lisa had been in school, and in none of those pictures was she pregnant. As far as the family knew, Lisa had never been pregnant and her brother was very angry that we would believe anything that Lisa had to say. According to Lisa, he had raped her also. Because I was not a case manager, I rarely ever found out who succeeded during improvement periods. At times, I was glad that I didn't know. I had done the best I could with this most unusual situation and this now became the job of a case manager. Only time would show if Lisa would make it as a mother. As with everyone, she would be given every opportunity.

~

Not My Baby

Millie wasn't a young woman, however she required a payee due to her mental disability. She moved frequently and never stayed very long in one place. Her mental status also made her a prime target for other transient people. Because of her situation, she didn't know she was pregnant until she arrived at the hospital and also because of her situation, she didn't believe the nurses had given her the right baby. Her infant was African American and Millie was positive she had never slept with a "black man". A day or so later, she walked away from the hospital and left the newborn behind. We were able to locate an appropriate family member who was willing and able to care for the little one, but she was afraid of Millie because of her mental health problems. A judge gave legal custody of the infant to the State and physical to the family member. CPS had to show an effort was made to reunite the family, provide what help Millie would take, and give her the opportunity to visit her baby.

She had one visit and it went something like this. The Aunt agreed to bring the baby down to a car if Millie wanted to see the baby. So on a Tuesday, Millie's Aunt took the baby boy and walked from her third floor apartment, down the stairs and to a car that belonged to a stranger. When Millie saw that the baby was the same one as in the hospital, she took a brief glance and declared that the people she was living with were members of the Ku Klux Klan and would kill "that thing". Her remarks were frightening. After publishing in the paper for the father and getting no response, the baby had a home with extended family. Times like these helped me to have faith in serendipity, God's intervention, or whatever you might believe. Millie's future would always be shifting and there was nothing to keep this from happening again.

𝜄

Helpless

Children with mental or physical disabilities are the most vulnerable to abuse. Some do not speak, and those that do, often do not comprehend their situation. Society has moved from using the words "mentally retarded" or a slow learner" to the term thought to be more kind, "lower functioning". These children often come from a family that may have more than one parent with a disability. Mary and Annie were children that had more than one disability and also had "lower functioning" parents. Annie was supposed to be in a wheelchair due to cerebral palsy, but often it was left behind in an abandoned house. Years ago, the State had paid for surgery on her legs, but no one had taken her back for follow up appointments or kept the braces on, and her legs had reverted back. We had ever heard her speak and so assumed she could not talk. Mary was somewhat higher functioning than her sister, but difficult to understand and quiet. Both girls were dirty and kept uncombed hair. Their mother Linda was mentally disabled and getting checks for herself and the girls. She understood some things, but mostly on a child's level. Their father was the payee and managed the money. I use the term 'manage' loosely because he used it primarily for alcohol and women. Linda said that Fred gave her one hundred dollars a month and they were homeless because that was all they could afford. In actuality, the family was receiving approximately two thousand dollars and could have been living in a nice home or apartment. The parents had met in foster care when they were children and so Linda trusted Fred and Fred alone. After all, hadn't they been through the same things?

When I found them, they were living in a car, but quickly pointed to a relative's empty house and called it home. As I was talking to Linda and the girls, Fred took off running. Fortunately for me, the police were patrolling the neighborhood and grabbed him as he was going into an abandoned house. In a neighborhood of abandoned homes, it's easy to jump from one to another in a matter of minutes. The police held him until I could ask him a few questions, and because I still believed they lived in the house I had been shown, they walked away that day. Linda had walked me through that house, told me where everyone slept, and while she was vague about some things, I assumed it was a mental delay and not deception.

After that day, the girls stopped going to school and disappeared. Sometimes I would find a school paper with one of the girls names on it or a piece of clothing. Once I found a bucket they had been using for a toilet in an empty building nearby. My concern was not only for their living conditions, but there were allegations Fred had sexually abused an older daughter and could be sexually abusing the two younger girls.

A computer search revealed over 20 past reports or investigations and a family that was transient between counties. Both the father and mother were in their late forty's and some thought they were related. The foster mother was deceased and there were no records. What reports I could find, suggested possible incest and numerous allegations of inadequate housing. Many days on my way home, I drove through the neighborhood hoping they might be outside.

Approximately six months later, a call from police sent another worker out to bring in the mother and daughters. They had been found in an abandoned house and were taken to the city mission. A protection plan was completed and the father was not to have any contact with the girls. He could talk to the mother on the street while they were in school and even that was worrisome. I had long since notified social security and had him removed as their payee. Both girls were given checkups and it was only after months of living in clean conditions, and having a somewhat normal life, that Annie began to speak a few soft words. While Mary's forensic interview had no findings, Annie was talking and the things she was saying were beyond belief. She spoke about a basement and movies and her sister touching her. Fred was in control and he had been making porn involving his wife and children. Police searched the house and could not find any videos or pictures and once again, we were close, but not enough for criminal charges.

I will never forget the day I took a call from a man who was upset about something he had seen. He told me about a man named Fred who owed him money and a meeting at the mall. Fred had told this man he didn't have the money, but in his van was something he would like even better. This caller told me he had gotten into the van with Fred and was shown a video that contained two young girls and their mother in sexual situations. He was disgusted and so upset he felt he needed to call. With the number of abandoned homes the family had hidden in, the hard evidence could not be found, but Annie continued to talk and she stuck to her story. Not only did she stick to the story, but she began to elaborate and her bravery gave Mary the strength to begin to talk also. I believe that Linda knew it was wrong, but she had been told it was her responsibility to teach the girls about sex. Did Fred give her a choice? I didn't know, but after many years the girls were safe and would never have to be around this monster who was called their father.

Sometimes persistence, team effort and faith all come together and you can only hope the damage done is not beyond repair. In the end, I didn't know if a Judge would let Linda raise the girls, but I did know that for the first time Annie and Mary were getting medical treatment, an education and had a home that most of us took for granted.

TWO ARRESTED FOR EXPOSING KIDS TO DRUGS, PORNOGRAPHY

April 23, 2011 @ 12:00 AM

LACIE PIERSON
The Herald-Dispatch

Two people were arrested Thursday after authorities said they allowed their children to be exposed to drugs and pornography. ************************, 47, and ******************, 48, were arrested and charged with child neglect after Cabell County Child Protective Services alerted officials to suspicious activity in the home according to a criminal complaint filed in Cabell County Magistrate Court Thursday. When West Virginia State Troopers executed a search warrant Thursday at the ********residence, they found marijuana, straws containing "a white powdery substance" and a DVD containing pornography in the bedroom of one of the

couple's three children, the complaint said. In the complaint, one of the children referred to another woman, who the child said the parents let sleep in her bed while the child slept on the floor where the drug para-phernalia was found. The child also referred to seeing the woman use drugs. In addition to the drugs and pornography in the home, troopers also reported finding rotting food, garbage throughout the residence, a roach infestation, a clogged toilet and "very offensive odors" throughout the residence. *********County CPS workers took custody of the children at the time of their parents' arrest. The **************** were incarcerated at Western Regional Jail Friday night. No bond had been set.

Part 6

~

Sticks and Stones

"I was angry about the fact that my father would beat my mother on a daily basis, that my mother would take it in turn and beat on me. I was an abused child. I was mad about all those things, very bitter and very angry".

-Rick James

Just Up The Road

Some think that child abuse and neglect is a problem caused by poverty. While to some degree this might be the case, there were plenty of wealthy people who felt their children needed to be perfect. In order to keep up appearances, they had to have well-mannered, faultless children. These children became pawns, and homes would sometimes consist of "her children", "his children" and "their children". Often, it was the child that rebelled or acted out that became the victim of the controller. If you couldn't pretend to be the perfect child, you would be made to be the perfect child.

Cheryl brought Michael into the office with bruises on the tops of his ears. Having just been to a conference on bruises and injuries, I knew ears had very few blood vessels and bruising took a lot of force. Cheryl told me she had went to her ex-husband's to pick up the children and Bill had come out calling her names and telling her how awful Michael had behaved. According to her and Michael, Bill had stepped up on the running boards, leaned inside the SUV, and continued to cuss and yell. She told him to get out and began to move the car. He continued and so she moved more, leaving him lying in the gravel. This is the part that appears to be the truth. The part about Cheryl trying to murder him and gunning it was his extended version.

After Cheryl got home, she saw the bruises on Michael and asked him what had happened. Michael told her his Dad had cornered him about fighting with his sister and was also angry because he wouldn't wear the clothes he had bought him. When he wouldn't stop watching television when told, his father had become angrier and Michael had shouted that he didn't want to come back anymore. To avoid his father's anger, he had ran and hid behind the plant in the corner. Bill had grabbed him by the ears and pulled him out just as Cheryl had arrived.

According to Michael and his sister, their father liked to have "board meetings" and if you didn't listen, you were "having a meeting with the board". I was told this replaced the use of a belt, which was referred to as "earning your stripes", or a similar business term. At the time, Michael had no other marks on his body and would not be visiting his father for a while. This gave me time to figure out the truth and to write a report for a family court judge. Individuals in custody or visitation battles often make CPS reports against each other in order to interfere with each other's rights. In these situations, family court judges will often request our unbiased investigation into both sides of the family. The situation between these two divorced parents was volatile.

I needed to interview Bill's children by his first wife and also his current wife's children. Liza was a very petite, mousy woman that seemed easily intimidated and always agreed with her husband. I expected since I had already had a phone conversation with Bill, that the other children would remain quiet. It was just procedure when I showed up at the schools and saw the kids individually. The oldest son, of this wealthy man, was much like his father and expressed anger that I was there to see him. Bill, Jr. was not interested in talking to me and further stated that he and his father often went golfing together. So far, nothing was any different than I had expected. Leaving the high school, I drove to the elementary school to see the children that belonged to Liza, (Bill's step-children). The little girl said nothing, but the young boy who was close to Michael's age was talkative. Josh admitted that he had tried to warn Michael not to do things or he would have a "board meeting". I asked Josh if he had ever had a "board meeting" and very nonchalantly he stood and pulled his sweatpants down on one side. On his upper left buttock, Josh had long, thin bruises that appeared to match that of a board or belt... unless of course he had fallen on the edge of something and fallen twice. I tried not to react and told Josh I wanted to get some pictures and needed to ask someone to bring me a camera. He went back to his classroom and I called my Supervisor to let her know my findings and to have a camera brought to the school. We were both surprised by the bruises on Josh and knew this was going to get ugly.

I would have to go to this man's home and do a "protection plan". A protection plan is basically an agreement between two parties, CPS and the client(s), that they will or will not do something for seven days until further investigation could occur. In this case, due to the lack of any other family in the area, I needed to ask the family to not use any corporal punishment. This agreement is totally voluntary, but a refusal gives us the option of contacting the prosecutor for further advice. One option, the last option, is to remove the children and take them into protective custody. This is what many people believe is our goal in Child Protective Services. In reality, it is traumatic for children, requires a court order, medical and clothing vouchers for each child, and finding a home that has room or is appropriate for each particular child or siblings. This is not easily done, as people assume. It's not "snatching and grabbing" and it's not something that a CPS worker chooses to do on their own. There is a lot of waiting, paperwork, finding homes, packing, moving, and sometimes waiting for law enforcement to assist.

It was later in the afternoon when I drove up the private road and parked in the circular drive at the large brick home. I was welcomed as if I was Mr. Wise's best friend and someone who would surely agree with him that nothing had occurred. When I confronted him about "board meetings", he was clueless and said any boards that may have existed had been broken or thrown out. This was not a big surprise to me. Bill then tried an intimidation tactic by trying to show me bruises he said he had on his own behind. According to him, he and his stepson Josh, would jump up in the air and bump hips when a player made a touchdown on television. I looked at Bill and firmly told him that I didn't investigate adults, didn't want to see his behind and that it was impossible for a man that was six foot tall, to jump and bump hips with a four foot child. Furthermore, it would not produce bruises that were linear. Bill's story then changed to Josh possibly getting bruises at a friend's house playing football, but he couldn't be sure. He knew nothing about how Michael had gotten bruises on his ears and he was adamant that he had only called for him to come to his mother's car. He then proceeded to make the children stand in certain places for his own reenactment. He was attempting to place himself nowhere near the plant and swore he had never pulled Michael from a corner. This man's body language was frantic and he was visibly attempting to control his temper. I explained that if he wasn't willing to leave the home, (and I knew he wouldn't), that I needed him to sign a protection plan. Well of course, he was not signing anything. I then told Bill it was only asking him to not hit, grab, or use an instrument of any kind, nor to ask to see his children by his ex-wife until I could complete my investigation. If he didn't agree to sign, I would have to contact the

Prosecutor and have the children removed. Bill reluctantly and feverishly signed. His controlled emotions were slipping and his eyes were hard and livid.

I left and went home to relax and breathe again. As a social worker, even though we may be afraid, upset or angry, we try to keep a calm demeanor. It wasn't unusual for me to drive out of sight and then either call my Supervisor or simply sit and utter a few choice words. Home was a refuge and when I opened the door, the world I worked in was left behind.

In a few weeks, I was subpoenaed to family court and both Cheryl and Bill were there with their high dollar attorneys. It felt as though piranhas were circling and I was the bait. Bill's attorney was a female who was known for chewing people up and spitting them out in the courtroom. Fortunately, this family judge had read my investigation and upheld my findings. Bill's attorney was told to "sit down and shut up" and Bill was ordered to have parenting in his home and counseling before Michael could return. Unfortunately, Josh changed his story and wasn't talking about the "board meetings" anymore. I was only able to substantiate findings of abuse in the case of Michael.

Mr. Wise, however, wasn't finished with me and decided to file a grievance. How dare I find him guilty of anything and he wanted a fight. Before the hearing, he showed up at the office and wanted to speak with me. I decided not to bring him back to my desk, but to walk to the lobby with a security guard. My instincts were correct, and with the security guard only 10 feet away, Mr. Wise decided he wanted to show me how he had grabbed Michael's ears and so he reached his arms out for my own ears. Instinctively, I stepped back and said "Stop, don't touch me". He stared at me and said, "Wow, that was scary... you scared me". I reminded him that I was not his son, nor was I his son's height and he needed to leave. He was escorted from the building and ended up losing his grievance. This was the first time anyone had ever tried to put their hands on me and I fought back tears as the adrenaline subsided.

~

Playing Yahtzee

For whatever reason, there are a lot of exasperated parents that see beating their children as righteous punishment and have little or no remorse. Some new parents are easily frustrated and don't know how to parent. Others take out their anger at life, on their child. The law in West Virginia states it is okay to whip your child as long as you don't leave marks or bruises. As a rule of thumb, if a red mark lasts longer than twenty seconds, you have whipped too hard. Spanking is a much debated subject, but it's important to realize there will come a time when it doesn't work anymore. A positive reward for positive behavior requires more work, but is worth it. Praise your child for good behavior and explain to them why certain behaviors are wrong. Discipline can be time-out, sitting on a step, sitting on a bed, no toy or a small chore for a young child. Older children love their cell phones, computers, friend time, television and games. If you find out what your child values, you will know what personal rewards will be most effective. This not only works for children, but adults as well.

Sixteen year old Emily was still living with her parents when she found out she was pregnant. Shortly after the infant's birth, she moved in with the child's father, Jason. The problem was Jason had his own life and spent a lot of time at his friend's apartment "making music". Her support had disappeared when she moved away from her parents and now she had an absent boyfriend. Emily was alone with Michael all day and as he got older, he became a normal toddler, with the added frustrations a toddler brings.

Michael usually spent weekends with his paternal grandparents, but when they couldn't get a hold of Emily one weekend, they decided to just stop by. Emily was unusually reluctant but finally let them take Michael. It was only after they got home, and went to change his diaper, that they found bruises and blisters going up Michael's back and down his little legs. They did the right thing and took Michael to the hospital. Michael was so afraid of being hit, when his diaper was removed for photographs, he immediately began to cry. The police were called and went to Emily and Jason's, but no one was at home. An emergency worker

placed Michael with the grandparents until someone could figure out what had happened.

The next day, I was given this investigation and
needed to find out who had hit Michael. Had it been
the boyfriend/new father, the mother, or someone
else? Arriving at the home early the next morning, I
found Emily sitting outside on the curb. I asked to
speak with her about her son and so we went inside
the little house. Every room was clean and well
kept. In an attempt to get her to communicate with
me, I told her I understood toddlers could be
frustrating and asked her what things Michael did
that was upsetting. She said he would get into stuff
and so she put him in his highchair to keep him out
of things. He would be given finger foods and then
cry and throw them. I got the feeling Michael was
spending a lot of time in his highchair. When
Michael threw food, Emily said, "I spank him to
make him stop". I asked her if she would
demonstrate this, and so she pulled out a dining
room chair, sat down, and pretended to lay him
across her lap. She then proceeded to raise her arm
up and down, as if spanking him hard. Emily told
me she would first try on top of his diaper, but then

when he wouldn't stop crying, she would pull it down and continue to hit him with a wooden spoon.

There were no tears; Emily felt victimized by this child and his continued crying was unfair to her. I told her I needed her to be completely honest with me about what had happened and only then would I be able to help her. When asked where the spoon was she had used on Michael, she began digging through his toy box. She dug so slowly and methodically I knew it was not there. She supposed she might have thrown it in the trash. Since the trash had not been collected, I asked her to bring in the garbage and again, she slowly went through it and I knew it was not there. She finally confessed she may have taken one bag to a dumpster, but couldn't recall which one. I wasn't getting anywhere.

As time passed, doctor's reports stated Michael had been beaten numerous times and had old and new bruises. Again I talked with Emily and took a co-worker with me who had a firmer approach. I felt she might get further due to her years of experience. Nicole and I banged on a bedroom window to get Emily out of bed for the appointment. I asked Emily where she had been

Friday evening, when the police came to her home, and she told us they had gone to buy cigarettes and beer. Astonished and somewhat appalled, I said, "Are you saying that while your child was in the emergency room, you were out buying cigarettes and beer... why?" Her response was simple, "It was Friday night and we were playing Yahtzee". Never before had I interviewed someone who talked about their child being hurt and lacked remorse; Emily had a flat affect. She refused to give us any other details and the father said he had no idea what had occurred. According to him, he hadn't been at home, nor had he really been a caregiver for his child. Based on the information I had, I believed him.

Looking back through the family's history, I found another incident which had occurred when Michael was three months old. It said he had fallen out of a baby swing from the top of a flight of stairs. According to that report, Emily had been moving and had attempted to carry the baby down the stairs while still in the swing. As she began to walk down the stairs, he had fallen out. As a mother, I knew swings weren't stable when lifted and it was risky at best. I went back once more and asked her if there had been any other times Michael had gotten hurt, and the swing was now a walker, or maybe a high chair. Fearful that that this child would not live if allowed to return, I filed a petition to keep him out of the home and the investigation was given to city police detectives.

Detective Wells later showed me the video-taped interview with Emily. His questioning technique was diversionary. He would speak about unrelated topics and then would ask, "So you hit Michael about ten times?" and she would respond "yes" and then he would switch to another subject and then return to, "So you think you hit him maybe twenty times?" He continued to do this until he got to fifty and finally she said "no more than that".

This case went to a court worker and the Judge ordered parenting and supervised visits at the Department. Eventually, Emily got Michael back and I would be lying if I said I felt good about it. Hopefully, with family support and attention, Michael would be safe. Emily stipulated in Court to child abuse with injury and was found guilty. Even so, if she completed services and improved, she could have Michael back. In the future, any injury would be dealt with differently and could result in jail time. Emily would never be able to work in child care or with children in any other way for the rest of her life... but she could be Michael's mother. It was now two years later, and I decided to see if I could find Emily on Facebook. I found her posing with Michael in her arms and she had written, "Innocent until proven guilty". She and a friend were laughing and giving the camera the middle finger. Feeling sick, I stopped writing for the day.

Part 7

~

Friends in a Bottle

"Children are often the silent victims of drug abuse".   *–Rick Larsen*

Just Up The Road

Prescription drugs are the predominate drug problem in our area and it's an addiction that makes poor people poorer and depressed people even more likely to neglect their children. The pills, named like women: Xani, Lori, Oxy, Roxy and others, personify them as girlfriends or at least best friends. In addition to making problems disappear by sleeping the day away, they are easy money for those that take advantage of the addiction (including doctors). If a local pharmacy finds someone doctor shopping, the client then may make trips out of State in order to expand their territory or supply. The lack of a nationwide database, allows individuals to travel and bring back large amounts of prescription drugs. Often the "scripts" are good enough, since it's much safer to exchange paper.

Six year old children now know what "blunts" are, different pill colors, and the way pot smells. They may know where the plate is hidden used for crushing pills, what a glass pipe looks like and may have even seen their parents sniff powder through straws. Some children have told me about a "chemical smell" and others have heard the "crushing sound on the plate" after they have been sent to bed. Children are brighter than their parents give them credit for and many are angry or worried about their own safety. Some have had to call 911 when "mommy won't wake up" or sit in their car seats while a parent is passed out. Often a passing police officer or neighbor will find them alone. Drugs cause children to miss a lot of school, come to school dirty, hungry and or tired from parties that kept them awake. They are exposed to a criminal element and strangers who may hurt them in ways no one can imagine. Frequently, children who are babysitting themselves may wake up a parent and if angry, the child is at risk of being hit or beaten. Many have to find food on their own, dig in empty refrigerators or ask neighbors for something to eat. Asking neighbors for food will often lead to a CPS report. If the parent has been told we are coming, the pantry will be full and there is nothing we can do for the time being.

In this area, 5 out of 10 babies are born with drugs in their system. If the mother is going to a methadone clinic, it is not considered child abuse. It is also not considered child abuse to use drugs while pregnant, even if that infant ends up going through terrible withdrawal and having to be placed on methadone. Per law, child abuse can only occur after birth and not in the womb. Their withdrawal symptoms are based on a scoring system referred to as an abstinence score. The lower the abstinence score, the fewer symptoms of with-drawl. A score between 10 and 20 is indicative of a infant experiencing withdrawal symptoms that may include tremors, excessive crying, diarrhea, insatiable sucking of hands or fingers, and other things that no infant should have to face coming into the world.

Marijuana use is excused because "it will increase their appetite for the baby's benefit" or "help the pain of early labor". The consequences of marijuana use are having a baby born high, with potential respiratory problems and spending time in the NICU. Child Protective Services gets called when a child is born with drugs in its system or the mother has tested positive. Often a newborn showing signs of withdrawal will need treatment without anyone ever knowing what the mother has taken. Getting a parent to take responsibility for the infant's struggle is difficult and often people will say they have been set up or a mistake was made in the lab.

Drug abuse doesn't always mean that the parent is leaving their baby behind; it merely means that they will be required to have safety services in the home several times a week. If at any time, the provider or case manager feels that the client is not complying by shrugging off impromptu drug screens or not being home for appointments, a court petition is sent to the Judge. The petition asks the Judge to intervene based on the present situation, and to schedule a hearing in order to either get the client to comply or face the consequences. Typically, the family is then given ninety days to show improvement or if the worker feels that the infant or child is in danger, the worker has the legal right to remove the child from the home. When it comes to drug abuse, it usually doesn't take long to see if a parent intends to improve or is unable to put their child first.

I've witnessed a parent come to a supervised visit and struggle to hold their head up. They may ignore the infant, talk on their phone, roll cigarettes, or even fall asleep. Some spend so much time on the cell phone and cursing; they are warned and then told to leave. They are observed through a two-way mirror and a worker can immediately walk into the room and give a warning or cancel the visit all together. This information will then go in a court summary and the Judge is made aware of what has occurred since the previous hearing. We desire for parents to make it and to raise their own children. We celebrate their successes and mourn their failures because of the child. If they choose drugs over parenting, protecting the children will always come first.

This area is fortunate in that there are inpatient facilities that allow a mother to take an infant or child with her and parent while going through rehabilitation. There are also inpatient facilities for men. Neither place is for anyone so seriously addicted that hospitalization is necessary for withdrawal. In those situations, a family member may be able to assist while the parent goes through treatment and then they can move down to outpatient counseling. It is a long process and only the individuals willing to sacrifice drugs for their child are able to make it. As with any addiction, a whole new lifestyle is necessary; friendships, location, depression, stress and individual reward systems all need to change. The following is an editorial written a few years ago concerning the problem in this area.

Editorial: We must find ways to reach pregnant addicts

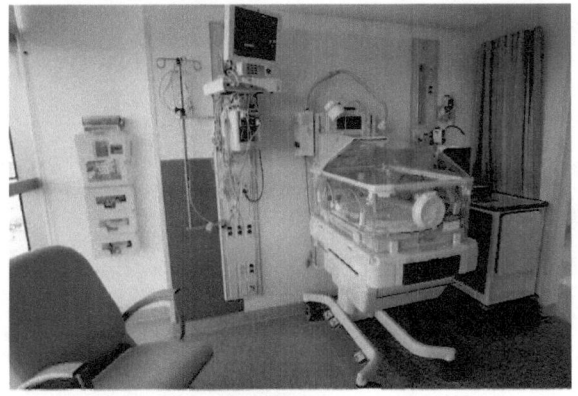

Lori Wolfe/The Herald-Dispatch
March 22, 2009 @ 12:00 AM

The problem of drug addiction in the Tri-State affects even the newborn. An article in the March-April issue of the West Virginia Medical Journal, published by the West Virginia State Medical Association, details the growing problem. Three physicians looked at newborns diagnosed with neonatal abstinence syndrome (NAS) discharged from Cabell Huntington

Hospital in calendar year 2005. NAS is a group of symptoms caused by neonatal withdrawal from maternal use of narcotics. According to the article, 48 newborns were diagnosed with NAS in 2005, 40 of whom required time in the Neonatal Intensive Care Unit (NICU). The majority of the mothers had poor or inconsistent prenatal care. Opiates were the most common substance found in mothers, while babies most often tested positive for methadone. Thirty-four of the mothers were found to continue illicit drug use while pregnant, while another eight were seen in a methadone clinic for a history of abuse. Most of the newborns required weaning with methadone. The majority of study cases were funded by Medicaid, mostly by West Virginia. The article has much more detail about the babies and the mothers. While the study focused on the 48 babies discharged from Cabell Huntington in 2005, it also noted that the number of babies with NAS in 2007 had increased to 70. Final numbers for 2008 have not been compiled, but it likely is higher, said Dr. Robert Nerhood, chair of the Department of Obstetrics and Gynecology at the Joan C. Edwards School of Medicine at Marshall University and one of the three doctors doing the study. Babies born to drug-using mothers usually are not malformed, but they tend to have attention deficit difficulties and learning disabilities, Nerhood said. Nerhood said the researchers don't know what happened to most of the babies they studied. The study noted that 23 of the 48 went home on outpatient methadone treatment. It also said 31 went home from the hospital with their mothers, five with relatives and 11 to foster care. One returned to the emergency department nine days after discharge with cardiopulmonary arrest and died three days later. "Drug-abusing pregnant women should be reached as early as possible, but that can be difficult because they might not open up to their physicians about their drug use", Nerhood said. "The approach has to be a nonjudgmental fashion, without threat. Women using drugs must be reached early in the pregnancy, while their maternal feelings are greatest. Unfortunately, addiction sometimes overwhelms the motherhood instinct," he said. With the increased attention to the effects of drug use in the Tri-State, the whole matter of babies born to drug-abusing women has not gotten much attention. But it has to. Drug abuse affects people of all ages, from elderly victims of crimes perpetrated by drug users to the unborn children of drug-abusing mothers. Nerhood said West Virginia has few rehabilitation centers. One of the maternal fetal medicine physicians at the Marshall University medical school is working with an agency for a joint program to help drug-abusing pregnant women, he said. Soon, The Healing Place Huntington will open a residential program to help drug-abusing men overcome their addictions. A similar treatment center for women is next in The Healing Place's plans. For far too long, the Tri-State ignored its drug problem. At one time, the drug problem was seen as confined to one or two areas, with most of the violence occurring among dealers and users. Since the four teens were killed in the predawn hours of prom night nearly four years ago, it has become obvious the problem is much larger than many people originally thought. Because the problem was out of sight and out of mind for so long, West Virginia has had few systems to deliver the help people need to overcome their addictions to prescription painkillers, cocaine, heroin and other drugs.

Although the state is facing a budget cut back next year, it cannot ignore this problem any longer. It's not just the adult users who are suffering. Innocent children, whether they are born addicted to their mother's drugs or if they are toddlers living in deplorable conditions, are affected, too. As Nerhood said, the Tri-State area has limited options for pregnant women seeking detox. Also, drug-using pregnant women don't have good support systems, he said. They need a good support system from the community: a place to sleep, access to food and access to transportation. The Healing Place has been in the works for several years. A similar effort will be needed to help our smallest victims of the Tri-State's drug problem.

~

Boo Boo

Many individuals feel that they are smarter than the average user or seller and are truly imaginative in finding ways to hide their drugs. While some social workers take the attitude where there's smoke there's fire, I tended to give individuals the benefit of the doubt until they proved me wrong.

With some, it took longer to discover drug use, especially the really crafty ones.

The Kessler family consisted of a young couple who had an adorable, blonde-headed, three year old son. Their problem was that he was an incredibly smart and talkative little boy. He was telling extended family that mommy had a "boo-boo" and this was worrisome. The grandparents were reporting that his mother had needle marks and had left a tourniquet in the bathroom at their home. Mandy had told them it was a drawstring that had come out of her sweatpants. I needed to try to find out if there was anything happening or if the grandparents were just being over protective. I tried talking to Trevor in his room, but he wanted to play with his toys while a little puppy ran in and out. Not getting anywhere with him, I went back to the living room and read my report to Mandy. She showed me her arms with needle scars on her inner elbow, but explained she donated blood for extra money. This was not unusual for people in a tough spot and even though I could see scarring, there were no visible track marks, or marks running up and or down a vein. She had no marks between her fingers or her toes and when I asked about Trevor saying she had a "boo-boo", her response was their new puppy's name was Boo Boo. While Mandy used the puppy's name, the child didn't seem to pay much attention to the dog or call it anything. I asked her about leaving a tourniquet and she told me the same story about forgetting a drawstring in her mother's bathroom and Trevor retrieving it.

At this point, I didn't have much to go on and there wasn't any past criminal history. I was surprised when I called the Drug Task Force and was told that the home was under surveillance and that the mother's routine included putting the child in a car seat and taking long drives into the city. While she was being followed, they had yet to see anything occur. I didn't have enough to go on and would have to close my investigation. I felt somewhat better knowing law enforcement was still keeping an eye on Trevor.

A few months passed before I saw the Kessler's pictures in the newspaper and on the jail website. Their car had been stopped at the greyhound bus station and even though a canine dog had hit on it several times, they couldn't find anything. Officers continued to look and finally found a bag of Skittle's candy in the car. While it appeared to never have been opened, a closer examination showed each Skittle had been cut open with a razor and had an Oxycontin inside. The stickiness of the candy had made it easy to push back together and the bag was resealed.

I learned later the dog had been purchased after Trevor started saying "Mommy had a boo-boo". Mandy needed a cover for his innocent words and was creative. The drugs had come from Detroit and into the station, by a courier, who was also arrested. This wasn't always the case and often a person would turn around and head immediately back. Fortunately for Trevor, he had extended family that loved him and could care for him while his parents were incarcerated. He wouldn't have to see mommy's boo-boo's anytime again soon.

Deputies find OxyContin in candy bag

Lori Wolfe/The Herald-Dispatch

Sheriff's deputies intercepted a supply of OxyContin on Tuesday, March 31, 2009, in Huntington. They found 190 pills hidden inside of a Skittles candy bag.

April 01, 2009 @ 02:44 PM
CURTIS JOHNSON
Herald-Dispatch.com

Sheriff's deputies intercepted a supply of OxyContin on Tuesday night. They found 190 pills hidden inside of a Skittles candy bag, according to criminal complaints filed in Cabell County Magistrate Court. Those arrested were ******************, 20, of Detroit, along with **************** and *******************, both 26 and of Milton. All were charged with two counts of felony possessing a controlled substance with intent to deliver. Bond was set at $100,000. The criminal complaints state the Cabell County Sheriff's Drug Unit received information about an Oxycontin shipment headed for Huntington. The *************were scheduled to pick up the pills and a man at the Greyhound Bus Station in **********. Deputies spotted the ************ arrive in a white Oldsmobile, the complaints state. A man got into the vehicle about 11 p.m. Tuesday. Deputies followed the vehicle and stopped it in the 2400 block of 5th Avenue. The complaints state ************* gave deputies consent to search the vehicle. A canine deputy alerted his fellow officers to the vehicle's trunk. Deputies searched the vehicle and found the sealed Skittles bag. It contained 150-80 mg pills and 40-40 mg pills. The suspects were transported to the Western Regional Jail.

⁓

Out on the Ridge

Some kids grow up with grandparents instead of parents; the same grandparents who used drugs when their parents were young. Of course, who needs pills more than the elderly and who is less conspicuous than someone with a cane or an oxygen tank? The Carter's lived on top of a twisting mountain road and while still drug users, they were quite different than those living in the city. It's much easier to hide a drug addiction if the police aren't driving by doing safety checks.

Sam was ten years old and his father, James, was an addict. His mother had taken off with a truck driver years ago and so Sam was left to be raised by a grandmother who provided pills for her husband, daughter and her son-in-law. The combination of Xanax and Oxycontin caused arguments involving broken glass, knives and bats breaking windshields. Sam survived by soiling himself and hiding in his grandmother's room. This family was going through four prescriptions of Oxycontin and Xanax a week and were stilling running out. The grandfather told me he bought extra from people just driving by and I laughed. Drive-by's didn't occur on top of a ridge, in the middle of nowhere.

As the fighting got worse, an emergency worker was called after the Aunt stabbed her husband and Sam had called 911. By the time the police arrived, the family had cleaned up the blood and promised to remain calm the rest of the evening. The next day I was assigned the family and decided to take another worker along due to the violence in the home. Sam had been soiling his pants for years and his grandfather would punish him with a whipping. I soon learned that it was normal for the grandfather to go through withdrawal and have seizures on the living room floor. When Sam wanted to call 911, he was told to "Just let him lay there for a while and he will come around". This was something that would have been upsetting to an adult, much less a child.

Trying to find another family member who wasn't involved in drugs was a challenge, but I knew Sam was terrified and needed out of this home. Ultimately, a different Aunt came forward and the home appeared to be appropriate. She had other children and lived near the school. Sam seemed to be happy being with his cousins and after just one week, the soiling stopped. His father James denied using drugs and tried to get visits. A Judge gave him visits at McDonalds, a public place with cameras. It was the Aunt's responsibility to bring him to the visits and wait each week. It didn't take long for James to prove he had no desire to change. He was showing up at visits under the influence and starting fights. Soon afterwards, I got a call from an irate girlfriend saying James was injecting drugs into his penis and this was the reason we couldn't see marks. I had never heard of this and so searched on the internet and found it was an ideal spot for various medications. This prompted me to call my Supervisor to let her know this investigation was something most suited for a Supervisor and we both laughed. These experiences help to refine our warped sense of humor.

During this time, Sam missed his grandmother terribly and so she moved to a place where she could raise him by herself. Sadly, she didn't live much longer and Sam was returned to his grandfather. Life moved on and I was no longer involved with this family. Some kids are the innocent victims of the bad choices made by those who are suppose to love and care for them.

The Community Car

Drugs in the home are dangerous when a child or teenager wants to try a few themselves. The first time I saw Shawn he was lying in a hospital bed on life support. The doctors had never thought about doing a drug test on a child, and so when he was admitted, it was thought he had experienced a seizure or respiratory problems. Shawn was only 10 years old and luckily within a day or two, his breathing tube came out and he was able to say that he had taken a blue pill and a red pill. According to him, he had found them in the front yard in a plastic baggie and wanted to try them. I didn't believe they had been lying in the front yard, especially when drug abuse ran in the family and mom's boyfriend was visiting from Detroit.

Pleading with Shawn was useless and so I tried to impress upon him how lucky he was to still be alive. Lovenna's boyfriend came in from Detroit to visit fairly often and yet she couldn't explain what he did for a living or how he could afford to make the trip so often. It was during one of these conversations that I learned about the "community car".

In my efforts to open this mother's mind to the possibility that her boyfriend might be involved in drugs, I asked if he was flashing money, if he brought gifts and what kind of car he drove. Lovenna told me that he drove the "community car". I had no idea what a "community car" was and curiosity got the best of me. She explained that there was a large, older model maroon car that sat in the neighborhood or "hood" and whoever needed to use it, could put five dollars in it, use the key and then park it nearby when they were finished. It was amazing how creative people were when the need arose.

Shawn came home within a few days, and while this had been a very serious situation, I couldn't prove anything without him telling the truth. I was grateful Shawn was alive and we could only pray this experience would be enough to keep him away from drugs for the rest of his life.

/ν

The Glass Pipe

Kids are so much smarter than their parents give them credit for and even when they are threatened with silence, a good social worker can help them disclose without betraying their family. My approach to drug use was to begin with cigarettes because they are legal and socially acceptable. If their mommy or daddy smokes cigarettes, what kind are they, or what does the cigarette look like? Do they smoke anything else?

What color is it and what does it smell like? Another question was to ask if they had to take any medicine and then follow with, do your parents take any medicine? Most parents try to keep their substance abuse hidden from their children, but this is not always the case. Children are well aware that their parent may have a secret place or notice when they go somewhere and come back acting "funny or weird". Often they may notice that money is exchanged for pills or weed and also know with which neighbor or person. Just as the children want to tell about their friends, they find it simple to talk about mom or dad's friends and when they usually come over. Many clients lived in public housing and this made it easy for a child to know how many doors away or at which door number the friends were located. In the country, a child may be able to describe the color of a house or trailer and tell me how to get there or what it was close to. Sadly, some children were upset when their birthday or Christmas toy disappeared and were anxious for someone to step in and make their parents stop.

When I used, "Does daddy smoke?" with twelve year old Jimmy, his answer was, "cigarettes and some-times a glass pipe". He then immediately told me to "Scratch that part out". I drew a line through it and we talked some more about the things that he and his father liked to do together. He told me about their special place in the woods where there was a big rock next to a creek. I asked what they did there and he told me that it was his job to gather the wood and put it on the rock and then his dad did some cooking. He explained it was not food, but smelled like chemicals". How a child knew what chemicals smelled like was a mystery to me, but those were his words and it may have been something he had overheard. He also told me about his father's friend who use to live with them, but was now in jail because of a fight.

After talking to my Supervisor, and asking for a deputy to follow me out this narrow dirt road, we found the little, cluttered house at the very end. It was surrounded by metal cans lined up in front of piles of junk, the kind of cans used for gasoline or kerosene. The officer knocked on the door and since there was no answer, we dodged the dogs, turned around and went back. Together we approached a nicer home at the beginning of the road and the gentleman explained that the State Police had been trying to catch his neighbor for years. He had allowed them to use his land to watch the house and deeply regretted selling the land to the family.

After thanking the deputy for his help, I was going to check with the State Police and call my Supervisor. I had serious concerns about this place being a meth lab and the child's exposure to toxic chemicals. My supervisor was adamant that I needed to wait and check the home; I was adamant it wasn't going to happen. Having been previously trained in meth-lab awareness, I knew this could possibly be a hazardous material situation, not something for an unprotected social worker.

The neighbor said sometimes the child's father picked him up from school and other times he rode the bus. I waited to see if Jimmy got off the bus that day and when he didn't, I drove away. My anxiety level was high because of what I was being told to do. Once more I felt I was being asked to put my life at risk by someone sitting in a comfy office. I was angry and knew that my days doing this were coming to an end. So far I had been to a home in which a worker had been murdered, opened a bedroom door and found two drug dealers sitting on a child's bed, opened a closet and found a person hiding from me and also been told that it was okay to go to homes where there might be felons with guns. This didn't include the violent dogs, verbal abuse and aggressive people. While some workers seemed to take this all in stride, I was quickly burning out and didn't know how to change it.

When Jimmy's father found out that I had been to school to talk to his son, he called and spoke to my Supervisor while I was out of the office. Dwight blamed his ex-wife for this report and said he was taking pills for a back injury. He told her we were free to come out anytime. Her words were, "he sounded very nice" and my thoughts were, "of course he did". After contacting the State Police and not getting any answers, my Supervisor reassigned it to someone she had convinced to go in the house. The other social worker reported the house was a mess, but she didn't see any signs of a lab. Yet again, a lack of information meant we had to close another investigation. I had believed what Jimmy had told me and knew a father smoking a glass pipe smelling of chemicals was not a good thing.

Two years later, this article appeared in the local paper and the men listed included Jimmy's father and the friend from jail. My fears were legitimate, but there wasn't anything I could have done at the time. Once again, "A whale always has to come up for air".

Two Jailed on meth charges

May 06, 2011 @ 12:00 AM

CURTIS JOHNSON
The Herald-Dispatch

West Virginia State Police arrested two men Wednesday who they allege were operating a meth lab just outside of********. ********, 52, and *********, 48, each were charged with felony operating a clandestine drug laboratory, said West Virginia State Police Sgt. J.P. Murphy. The arrest followed State Police receiving an anonymous tip that methamphetamine was being cooked at a residence on Bedford Chapel Road. Troopers arrived, searched the residence and found a lab in the bedroom. ************** was

**also charged with felony exposure of manu-
factured methamphetamine to a child, according
to Murphy and jail records. Murphy said a 14-
year-old child was present at the time. The
teenager was turned over to his mother, Murphy
said. **********, additionally was charged with
felony conspiracy, according to Murphy and jail
records. Both of the men also received another
unspecified felony charge, jail records state. The
two were jailed on separate bonds of $60,000.**

~

Pot and Potatoes

Justin's father, Michael, had just gotten out of
prison for selling large amounts of marijuana.
Justin, who was about ten years old, had been living
with his grandparents while his Dad had been
incarcerated. Now that Justin was back with his
father, there were concerns he was still selling or
using around his son. When I arrived at the single
wide trailer in the country, Mr. Hesson wasn't
happy I was there for the appointment. He was
antsy and kept looking out the window at his
neighbor's house. When his neighbor finally came
out, he opened the door and told him to have a good

day. While I attempted to have a conversation with him, Mr. Hessen's attentions were elsewhere. After his neighbor left, Mr. Hessen decided he would speak and told me he had gotten a job at a local steakhouse and was in charge of the baked potatoes. Even though Justin could describe how to get to certain trailers, and who the men were his dad was selling and smoking weed with, Mr. Hessen adamantly denied this was occurring and was angry. He threatened to send Justin back to his grandparents for saying such things, not realizing it only made him look guiltier. After ample time, the only thing he would confess to was occasionally smoking pot himself, and according to him, never around his child.

The law in the State requires that drug use not occur around children or affect your parenting skills. Otherwise, our hands were tied when it came to drug use; we were not law enforcement. After gathering some information, Mr. Hessen walked me to my car. Trying to leave on a friendly note, I turned and said "take care" and "try not burn your fingers". (Referring to the potatoes) He responded, "I don't burn THEM down that far". I began laughing and said, "I was talking about the potatoes". His face turned red and I laughed all the way back to the office, until I found a new screw embedded in my tire. Suddenly Mr. Hessen's unusual behavior made sense. I felt certain he had been signaling to the neighbor to proceed with a prearranged plan. Thankfully, it was repairable and I had made it back to town. Needless to say, I never went to that restaurant to eat potatoes or anything else for that matter.

~

The Big Dealer

Relationships are reciprocal, meaning that each person has to feel that it is to their benefit to be with the other person. The next two relationships are perfect examples and not unusual when a woman has a boyfriend that is a drug dealer. Dependency, occurs when the female has become accustomed to a certain standard of living and it is beyond reason to live any other way.

Rachel was a pretty, mother of three, who showed up at the office one day and sat at my desk with her children. She told me her boyfriend had been arrested for drugs and she didn't feel safe going back to the house where they had been living. Someone had busted in the front door and trashed the place after his arrest. Additionally, Rachel wanted me to know what a nice house it had been and how hard it was going to be to leave. I asked if she would return if we were able to get the door repaired and new locks properly installed. She said "No, I've found a friend to stay with, but the kids can't stay because of the landlord". She reasoned her only option was to put the children in foster care.

The children sat next to her, pleading and crying, as she told me that they were just too much to deal with right now. They were promising to be good and to help, but she stared straight ahead and waited. The children appeared dirty and unkempt while Rachel wore a designer jogging suit, sunglasses and shoes. With the help of a Supervisor, I began looking for a place for the family to live, a shelter of sorts, or the city mission if necessary. The longer I took to make phone calls, the more agitated Rachel became and eventually her cell phone rang. I overheard her telling someone, "she was trying to hurry, but we were taking too long".

I walked up front to get a Supervisor because it was beginning to look like this mother just didn't want her children. Approaching my cubicle, we both overheard her telling the kids that she just couldn't handle their bad behavior anymore and they needed to go. Neither one of us could believe what we had heard. The Supervisor explained if she didn't have family to leave the children with, and if we took custody of them, it would take a Judge's order and tremendous amount of work to get them back. She said she understood and again stated she needed time to get her life back in order. It was obvious she was attempting to manipulate the situation and really wasn't interested in help.

I still see the little boy holding his head in his hands, crying and saying, "this just isn't right, it isn't right". After completing the paperwork, I told her to say goodbye and leave. They continued to cling to her, pleading and crying and even though she hugged them, she never shed a tear. Rachel told them that she didn't want them to freeze to death, but she was strong and would be fine. It was a line that made me angry, especially when I had found them a place to stay. Rachel didn't like any of our solutions; she wanted to be on her own again.

As I drove them to a foster home, the sobbing was so intense; I eventually pulled over to pass out napkins for the runny noses and tried my best to console them. The children suffered miserably in foster care and so did the foster parents. The kids were angry with their mother and yet they loved her and wanted to be with her. Over the months, I watched as she came for supervised visits in order to get the kids back. Eventually, she brought a man with her, the drug dealer's brother and her new boyfriend. She now had a nice car, a place to live and more jewelry and shoes, and I was left to wonder what would happen when this man was gone.

Belinda had a different version of the same story. She lived with her five kids, all of which had different fathers and worked part time as a home health aide. For some reason she tended to prefer men that ended up in prison and the majority were drug dealers.

When I met Jamal, it was because of a report which said "Biscuit hit me". Jamal was four years old, shy, sweet and loving. Biscuit was the nickname for the newest baby's father and he didn't like

Jamal's father, who he had known before he went to prison. I went to visit Jamal at daycare and waited in an office while he washed his hands after lunch. He held back when the assistant held his little hand and walked him to me. Since he was so small, I knelt down on my knees to be on his level and very quietly asked him if he had any "boo- boo's"? His fingers found their way to his mouth as he stared at the floor. I knew he had a bruise from the report and so with the help of the assistant, I took a picture of his face, a picture of the bruise, and then quietly asked him what had happened to his bottom. He leaned into me and sat on my leg. Cupping his hands to my ear, he whispered, "Biscuit hit me". Social workers aren't perfect, we get angry, frustrated, upset, some-times say things we shouldn't, but the most imperfect person in the world would have wanted to protect Jamal.

I had to wait for his Belinda to get home from work in order to do a protection plan. Since I was also worried about running into "Biscuit", I requested police officers to meet me at the apartment complex. When they arrived and I knew that Belinda was home, we knocked on the door and the police quickly checked the stairs and kitchen. I sat down and explained to the mother why I was there and why Biscuit needed to stay away. She stopped listening, called him on her phone and told him to "get home". While she didn't believe this had happened, she also knew how Biscuit felt about Jamal's father.

When this large man showed up and walked into the room, it suddenly became very small. His presence filled the small living area and the tension in the air was palatable. Because Belinda refused to keep Biscuit away from his new baby, Jamal's grandmother agreed to take Jamal with the other children. A Judge would decide whether it was safe for Biscuit to be in the home.

Judge O'Connell was a favorite of social workers, with a reputation of being supportive and fair. As I took the stand that day, Biscuit's assigned attorney was there, but he was not. Belinda and her attorney were there and so the Judge proceeded to ask Biscuit's attorney why his client "Mr. Biscuit" wasn't there. The attorney responded that he thought he might be visiting his cousin "Mr. Croissant". This was my first time in this courtroom and I was surprised by the banter, especially after the atmosphere in other courtrooms was so austere. The Judge said "Don't butter me up", and then everyone laughed and settled down.

Belinda tried to tell the Judge that Biscuit was never at her apartment and her attorney asked if I had gotten the video tapes of the complex and reviewed them. This was the most ridiculous thing I had ever heard of and I found myself saying that "it wasn't my job to investigate videos". This brought a chuckle from the Judge, even though I hadn't intended to be funny. The mother told the Judge that she would keep Biscuit away from her kids and the Judge told her that if at any time we had suspicions that "Mr. Biscuit" was coming to the home or around the children, the children would be removed. She agreed, and while I didn't trust her, it wasn't long before Biscuit was arrested with drugs and went a way for a few years.

The grandmother had told me that there was a tin can in the kitchen full of money, but we were not police officers and could only pass along the information.

****************: **The 27-year-old from ************** was sentenced April 15. Ferguson ordered ********** to spend one to three years in prison.**

************ had pled guilty to two counts of attempting to commit a felony. An October 2006 grand jury indictment initially charged *********** with first degree possessing a controlled substance with intent to deliver.

Approximately one year later, I took a new report about a man beating a little boy at a neighborhood carnival and the mother wasn't doing anything about it. It turned out to be Jamal and once more his mother had chosen some loser instead of her son.

The overall problem is women looking for men with money, and men (especially previous felons), looking for single women so they can have a place to do business, eat, have sex and hide out. A single mother may wait for years to finally get into public housing. When she thinks she has found Mr. Wonderful, he moves in and doesn't lift a finger to do anything other than "odd jobs". Odd jobs can be anything from lawn care, selling stolen property, pawning it, and often dealing. If illegal activity occurs on government subsidized or government owned housing, the family can be evicted and not allowed to return. In other words, their names go on a restricted list and this means that the mother and children are then left without a place to live again. Mr. Wonderful turned out not so wonderful, but he can move on to the next female, because like Rachel, everyone wants something.

Just Up The Road

Part 8

⌒

People, Places and Things

"Do you consider yourself a blessing or just another person?"

-Jonathan Anthony Burkett

Before this job, I had never heard of Child Protective Services and so when a teenager threatened to call CPS on their parent, I knew they had previous experience. When some teenagers don't like parental rules, they will runaway or sneak out. If caught, they might say they were either "kidnapped", "grounded unfairly", or "thought they deserved a cell phone". Keeping an open mind, when talking to a teenager, is absolutely necessary if you want to get through to them. Nevertheless, there were times when I thought it would be easier to tell if a professional criminal was lying before a teenager. The difference between child protective services and youth services is that CPS protects a child against parents that are abusive. Youth Service's assists parents who have out of control teenagers and need help with parenting. Many times what appears to be a CPS investigation will turn into a YS referral, implying what appears to be parental problems are actually child behavioral problems. Youth Services offers a menu of services for parents to choose from and it definitely takes a special type of person to work with teenagers.

William was thought to be a teenager that was lacking supervision and possibly had other problems at home. In reality, he had chosen to skip school and his behaviors were soon going to get him removed from alternative school and sent to a juvenile detention center. His truancy and grades had not improved with this last opportunity and things weren't looking good. When I went to see William, his body posture was one of disinterest and irritation. He slouched back in his chair, glared sideways and folded his arms.

After attempting to build rapport with William, I decided to try a more practical approach. I grabbed a sheet of paper and asked William if he had any idea what he wanted to do with his life. Not surprisingly, he hadn't put much thought into this, and so for our purposes, it was assumed he would be making minimum wage in the future. I calculated if he was able to get 40 hours a week, William would be making approximately 250 to 300 dollars a week, for a grand total of about 1200 a month, or 14,400 dollars a year. I asked William how much he thought rent, utilities, food, transportation, insurance, fuel (if he had a car), clothing, cell phone and a little extra for a night out would cost. As most adults know, we live in a time in which no one can make it on minimum wage and my point was to show William the advantages of an education. Feeling satisfied that I had made a good point with my presentation, I asked William what he would do since he couldn't afford to live on this amount? His response was quick…he and three friends would live together and then they would have forty eight hundred dollars a month.

Well, what could I say? William knew how to add, multiple and had a plan. I smiled to myself as I left the building and knew William would somehow survive. He was going through the teenage angst of wanting to be on his own and his difficulties were not the fault of his parents.

Less anyone think that I believe teens are never abused or neglected, I have met many parents who were alcoholics, drug users, or just generally mean people. Domestic violence between partners is frightening to children and considered emotional abuse. It is difficult for some parents to grasp that their fighting has an effect on their children. Often the older children will become the protector of the younger ones, whether they call for help or help them hide. Because teenagers speak up or out, they are often the victims of being hit, the runaway that begs to not go home, or the child that a parent sends elsewhere to live. They either choose to become like their parent in order to get along, or they rebel and are kicked out. When placed with a foster family, they often thrive. It may take time for them to learn what the rules are, but once they understand that this family is going to follow through, they go on to graduate from high school and sometimes even want to go to college. While many young adults end up going back to their birth families after turning eighteen, occasionally a few ask their foster families if they can stay. The need to belong and to feel a part of a family is essential for success; the lack thereof, is difficult to overcome.

The following article was published concerning two teenage girls I had done forensic interviews with and who had wanted us to believe they were being abused by their grandmother. The truth was they didn't like grandma's rules, curfews and chores and had found someone to hide them. I'm not sure why they thought their grandmother would not call the police or look for them. It is illegal to harbor or hide someone else's children, no matter what others may believe is occurring.

Three charged with hiding runaways in attic

April 22, 2011 @ 08:32 AM

CURTIS JOHNSON
Herald-Dispatch.com

Two men and a woman are charged with hiding two teenage runaways in an attic crawl space, according to court documents and a police report. The *********Police department arrested ***********, along with ***********. Each person was charged with two counts of concealment or removal of a minor child from custodian. They were jailed on individual $200,000 bonds. The Police Department's incident report listed the runaways as thirteen and fourteen years old. Both were girls. Criminal complaints charge both were found in a bedroom's attic crawl space at a house in the 900 block of Monroe Avenue. The complaints, which were filed in Cabell County Magistrate Court, charge the teenage girls had been listed as runaways in a

national database. None of those arrested had legal custody. Each of the adults were residents at the Monroe Avenue house, the complaints state. Those charged were incarcerated about 1:30 a.m. in the Western Regional Jail.

∿

Special Families

Every social worker has at least one family that they form a relationship with and it works for a while. My connection was with a large family whom I tended to understand the dynamics of and the kids were basically fine. We received a lot of reports because the neighbors would see the children outside and either believed they were being yelled at too much or needed to have shoes on their feet. I understood it was organized chaos and that they were basically happy children. After building a rapport with them, continued reports were approached with a comfortable, "just back to check on you again" attitude. They would say, "What now?" and I would update their lives in the computer. Occasionally, I would be asked to stay for dinner and was once invited for a night out with the mother. (Neither ever occurred) This type of relationship can only work for a while and then the family wants you to stop by anytime. Susan got so comfortable, she would call me at work to just talk or ask about my own family. It became so frequent; I was able to recognize her phone number.

At some point, I knew that I could no longer be totally impartial with this family and the friendship impeded my ability to be unbiased. I was still friendly if I ran into them, but when it came to CPS referrals, ethically they needed another social worker. A few months later, I smiled as I heard another social worker tell Susan that she appreciated the invitation, but needed to get home to her own family.

~

Hotel-Homes and Other Hideouts

Cheap hotels are rented by the night or week and are often hideouts for teenagers, drug dealers, meth labs, families in transition and prostitution. In order to understand the danger involved, you need to remember hotel rooms have only one way in and it's the same way out. They also have a bathroom for hiding and can be very dark. These hotels want to stay in business and so when police or Child Protective Services were looking for someone, a general description would usually get a room number. I've knocked on doors alone, or called for police assistance, especially when that inner voice gave me a warning. Either way, you never knew who or what you would find behind the dinged up metal door. Children usually don't disappear from school or their home without someone noticing. Occasionally someone staying in a hotel is aggravated by the noise coming from the next room or notices children being left alone. Managers' notice when children are running up and down the stairs during school hours and housekeeping notices when rooms never need cleaning and are beginning to smell. I found many families hiding out in these rooms.

We had two hotels that were notorious for murders, drug overdoses and most recently, meth labs. Knocking on doors, I was able to find a homeless woman with babies who had been missing and a teenager that I had dealt with the week before. Fate interceded and I got her back home. Other times people were less agreeable and when found hiding with hungry and dirty kids, they become even more hateful and angry. Realizing we weren't going to leave, they would eventually open their door. Often I would need to write a protection plan for the kids to be taken to the doctor or for them to get food sufficient for their needs.

It was funny when the news reported a pair of drug dealers forgetting their marijuana under a hotel bed and housekeeping finding it. The police were called and were waiting for them when they came back to retrieve it. Less funny were women who had children and worked out of their room as prostitutes. While children may have been asleep or appeared to be, they are put in danger for the sake of money. Strippers and some prostitutes can survive without the welfare system and make more money than many of us. This gives them the ability to live under the radar for quite some time. It's only when they are too tired, and forget to get the kids off to school, that we find them.

In addition to the dangers of hotel rooms, I have sat in an apartment and talked with a woman for an hour and then asked to see her home. Upon opening a door to a child's pink bedroom, I found two adult males sitting on one of the children's beds. I nonchalantly said hello, quickly exited, closing the door behind me. Once while checking for drugs, I opened a closet and a woman was curled up behind some clothing. I had no idea what they were afraid of, but it couldn't have been good. I quickly backed my way out, left with a forced smile and felt blessed to have made it to my car. There were many times I murmured a prayer of gratitude and went back to the office. I wasn't the only one and wouldn't be the last whose anxiety grew daily from these experiences.

ᴧ

Names

A rose by any other name is still a rose, but a child's name determines how they are thought of for the rest of their lives. Recently, I read about parents having their children removed for naming one Hitler and the others similar Aryan Nation names. In training, we heard about children with fanatical names which came from either a lack of education or a drug induced fantasy. I recall hearing about a female who named her baby, "Mary Juana", and a baby named, "Fe Male" with a long e, because that's what it said on the card in the bassinet. The mother had thought the baby came with a name. There was also "Va GIna", "Tequila" and others. In many instances, either an adoptive family changed the child's name or it was explained to the family that a child could not be named after alcohol or drugs. My personal experience was with an adult woman named, "Strohs Anna". After asking how she came to have such an unusual name, she explained her father's favorite beer had been Stroh's and so her mother had given her the name to surprise her father. Moments like those made me glad my parents didn't drink, do drugs or like V8. While I was a child of the Sixties and had known a few "Rainbows" and "Moonbeams", my parents were thank-fully conservative.

*

Pagers from Hell

Every two or three months, each worker got the little pager from hell. While it was an inanimate object, it took almost a year after leaving, to hear a microwave beep, a dryer buzz, or an alarm go off and not have my heart rate increase. In the beginning, if it was your turn for a week of pager, it wasn't so bad. Often the calls were inquiries that could be answered over the phone or minor things that required a signature after hours. When the system changed from risk and was replaced   with present danger calls, the pager became a beeping monstrosity that ruined your life for a week. When it went off, it could signify a child in the emergency room, a child needing to be removed from a home or abandoned children, and it always meant you were getting dressed and leaving. Sometimes the pager was kind and even the silence would become troublesome. Was it working, were the batteries okay, was it loud enough? When it did go off, it wasn't just once or twice; it was like the hiccups and stopped for no particular reason. You could hold your breath, and even try yelling, but it was only over when it was someone else's turn.

We all dreaded the little black attachment, with its accompanying luggage, car seats, camera's, cell phone and paperwork. If you really wanted to be brave, you tried going to a movie, dinner or party. I had the pager the day my oldest son got married and ended up leaving the reception. It was the first time it had went off all week. I must have tempted fate.

Just Up The Road

Part 9

Enough

"Consider how hard it is to change yourself and you'll understand what little chance you have in trying to change others".   *-Benjamin Franklin*

Just Up The Road

After so many changes in the system, the feelings of futility came to the forefront. It wasn't between us and the family anymore. Supervisors and higher ups disagreed about the definition of abuse and neglect and the desire to keep children safe didn't exceed the desire to make the States numbers look good. We had switched from being proactive to reactive and it seemed as if we only responded to children in dangerous situations, instead of helping families before it got that far. The new definition of danger felt arguably wrong and we were powerless to do anything about it.

The night before I gave my resignation, it was almost four o'clock. Another worker, whose case required the removal of two children, left instead of taking them to a kinship-relative placement. This was unusual and so I was sent to get a three year old and a baby from grand-parents who didn't have any idea what had went wrong or why it was occurring. I drove into the country and found a modest doublewide that was relatively clean and had five happy children inside. Knocking on the door, I asked to sit in the kitchen and talk to them. It was my job to tell them I needed to take two of their grandchildren. A granddaughter and a two month old baby grandson were to be removed and I had no explanation for the grandparents. I had been told to take them to an Aunt's home and it was a home that they were adamant was not fit for any child. No one had checked the Aunt's home and so there was a checklist to go through once I got there. Usually this was done ahead of time and background checks were thoroughly completed. As usual, things were being rushed, principally since it was the beginning of the weekend. I thought about what my own reaction would have been if a stranger had shown up and said they were going to take my grandchildren. What if that person wanted to place them in an environment I thought was bad for them? I understood their distress, and I had no idea what had happened or why I was there to do someone else's job.

I sat down, tried to explain, and listened as the grandfather said, "Over my dead body!" I telephoned the Supervisor who had sent me and put her on the phone with him. Her attitude made him angrier and so I walked outside on the deck. I did what I'd been trained to do; called for deputies to assist and thought about how much I'd grown to hate this job.

The deputies showed up and weren't use to working with Child Protective Services. Because the house looked fine to them, they wanted to see the Judge's orders before they helped me. Even though I had a verbal order, they were trying to get along with the grandparents and wanted a written order before they would assist me. I called my own Supervisor and she faxed a copy of the order to dispatch. This wasn't good enough for the shift commander and so he went back to get a paper copy twenty minutes away. I was left with an inexperienced deputy standing guard at the door and time passed slowly.

While waiting, the Assistant Prosecutor had gotten wind of the situation and started texting my phone. She wanted me to tell the family "to either let the children go or she would be issuing warrants for child concealment". It was approaching 6 o'clock pm. and I was angry at my co-worker for not doing her job, a Supervisor for not telling me what was going on, and law enforcement for making this even more difficult. I walked back inside where the deputy stood and nothing was being said by anyone.

While we had been waiting, the children's mother had shown up. I asked Jessica to please put the children's things together for them and she just looked at me. As quietly as possible, I told her that the Prosecutor wanted to charge them if they didn't let them go and I really didn't want that to happen. This triggered a response in the deputy and he turned on me. He tried to grab my arm and said, "There isn't any way that's going to happen, you go wait outside." My shock turned to anger and I responded "No, THIS isn't going to happen." He turned and walked outside and I now realized that I had no Supervisor, no other worker, no support from the family or law enforcement. I felt betrayed, dirty and alone, and so I did something more innate than protocol, I asked the mother to walk down the hall with me and away from the others. I needed this to be easier on her children and I needed her to help me so they would stop crying. I promised to take her with me to the Aunt's, while I did the safety check, but only if she promised to stay in the car. She agreed and together we were able to get the car seats in my SUV, and the children and supplies loaded. The young deputy stood silently watching.

Just Up The Road

The shift commander had yet to return and while my approach would not have been suitable in a non-family placement, it was a decision made by a heart who would have wanted the same respect. The feeling of being left all alone to do this made me feel justified. In my heart, I was daring anyone to say a word to me about how this had been handled.

Thirty more minutes over curvy, country roads gave Jessica and I time to talk and it was my first chance to understand what had been transpiring with her and her children. I encouraged her to be protective and to trust what her child had said about her boyfriend. She listened and I hoped in some small way it had went from one mother's heart to another.

The narrow, dirt road across from the gravel one, was behind tall grass and there was very little if any phone signal. I knew without a doubt, I would never have been able to have found this house alone and it was getting dark. As I made the sharp turn in the grass paved road, the brush subsided and I saw another doublewide with bags of garbage all around. I reassured the mother this was not part of the assessment and once again told her I wouldn't leave her children in an unsafe place.

Getting out of the car, I walked the carpet that led to the door of the trailer. Carpet is often used outside to cover the mud and keep it from going inside. The Aunt was in her forty's and smelled of cheap cigarettes. She said she had no idea I was coming or she would have cleaned up, and yet it was my understanding she had been told we would be there. Inside, there was a wall busted, cat litter sitting out, cat food thrown on the carpet, pill bottles sitting low and cigarette trays full of ashes on low tables. I tried in all fairness to recognize with a little time these things could be fixed, but there was no crib or bed for either child. I asked her where she was planning on the children sleeping and she showed me the dirty bed in the room with the cat food on the floor. I then asked where the baby was going to sleep and she told me "In bed with her". I explained that this was called co-habitive sleeping and was against the law. She said I should have brought her a crib. Once more I stepped outside and called a Supervisor with half a bar signal. I tried to explain the situation only to be abruptly told to, "Tell her to go buy one". I asked the

Supervisor what she wanted me to do with the children while this was going on and she was surprised I had them. When I returned to the Aunt with the request from the Supervisor, she screamed that she didn't have money to go buy a crib and "we could all go to hell". I thanked her for her time and told her there wasn't any need to curse. we were leaving.

This same Supervisor didn't have the home-finder's number, and so she told me to call the worker on call, and have him meet me somewhere. Jessica was relieved her children weren't going to the dirty home, but she also realized this meant a foster home. She preferred a foster home over the Aunt's home and I would have chosen the same. She was quiet as we went back down the mountain. When we got to the doublewide again, Jessica got out and her little girl began to cry. She hugged and kissed them both before we drove away and in order to take the three year olds mind off of leaving her mother, I told her that she was Dora the Explorer and that we were going on an adventure. We sang songs, as I drove the twenty minutes back to the office. I called my co-worker who was on pager and he called the home-finder before meeting me at the office. It was now 7:30 pm. and together we changed a diaper, gave the baby a bottle, and fed the little girl an apple left over from my lunch. The physical and emotional exhaustion was overwhelming and there was only one thing that kept me going... this was not the children's fault. They had been drug all over the county today and had been taken from their family. It was close to ten o'clock that night when we dropped them off at a wonderful foster home. I was grateful for my co-worker who was good with directions and I think he was glad that I was the one changing diapers.

The next day, the worker who had this case, made entries in the computer system which suggested there hadn't been any problems getting the children. The Supervisor who had failed to help me wasn't speaking to me and a complaint was made to the Prosecutor about the mother coming with me in the car. I sat at my desk and calmly entered every detail of the previous night. When I finished, I let my Supervisor, the other worker, and the Prosecutor know that I had put my contacts in the system, and they were welcome to read what had really happened.

~ 163 ~

Just Up The Road

My next correspondence began...“Thank you for the opportunity I've had to work here”.

~

Afterward

While it may appear that this book ends on a dispiriting note, it was not my intention. My purpose was to illustrate the frustrations and difficulties experienced after several years of working in this environment. The stories are a mere glimpse into the daily lives of a worker, a few families and several children. There were many homes in which a small improvement was all that was needed and often we met nice people who were gracious enough to let us in.

Nevertheless, the stories in this book are not the worst; there were others that wouldn't have been helpful. This is a career not meant for everyone and it is my hope others may benefit by having a better understanding of what the job entails. Social work is not for the faint of heart; it takes a lot of heart.

If you have time to help, be a mentor, volunteer at a Boy's or Girl's Clubs, donate toys at Christmas time or suitcases for foster children. One of my best memories was when Toys for Tots had leftover toys and donated them to CPS. We chose gifts and gave them to mothers who couldn't provide a gift for their child. It felt good to do something meaningful and simple.

~

Just Up The Road

Readers Discussion

High turnover rates of children and family social workers are caused by stress and feelings of being overwhelmed. What suggestions do you have for minimizing worker burnout?

After reading about some of the problems CPS workers encounter, what area or areas do you feel would be the most difficult for you?

What effects do you feel child abuse has on someone after they have grown up? Do you feel that there are some things that cannot be over come?

If you are feeling brave, look up the list of skin conditions and parasites mentioned in the book in order to see what they look like and how they are transferred.

The majority of the stories involved drug abuse or use and how it affected parenting. What do you think is the major cause for the increase in drug abuse in America today?

If you were assigned to create preventative measures to help ensure worker safety, what changes would you make and why?

Just Up The Road

www.ingramcontent.com/pod-product-compliance
Lightning Source LLC
Chambersburg PA
CBHW020424290526
45785CB00002B/711